To
Debbie

W[...] you love,
and
happiness

Anthony

CU00863437

What's the Point?

A GUIDE TO LIFE AND HAPPINESS

Anthony Peters

authorHOUSE®

AuthorHouse™ UK Ltd.
500 Avebury Boulevard
Central Milton Keynes, MK9 3BE
www.authorhouse.co.uk
Phone: 08001974150

Published by AuthorHouse 4/19/2012

ISBN: 978-1-4343-8917-6 (sc)
ISBN: 978-1-4670-2287-3 (e)

Dedication

This book is dedicated to all living beings with compassion and a sincere wish for all to be free from the sufferings of mind and resultant karma.

May all Buddha's, Bodhisattvas, Gods and holy beings continue to stay with us all and help turn The Wheel of Dharma so that we may all live in peace and happiness.

Acknowledgements

Special thanks to Simon Heighway, whose discussions with me are major influences in the contents of this text.

Thanks to <u>Geshe Kelsang Gyatso</u> et al. for giving us all the opportunity to live happier, more content lives through influential books such as;

- *Eight Steps to Happiness: The Buddhist Way of Loving Kindness*

- *Introduction to Buddhism: An Explanation of the Buddhist Way of Life*

- *Joyful Path of Good Fortune: The Complete Buddhist Path to Enlightenment*

Thanks also to Eckhart Tolle for sharing his enlightened knowledge in his books:

- *The Power of Now: A Guide to Spiritual Enlightenment*

- *Through the open door to the vastness of your true being*

Huge thanks to *Barefoot Doctor* for making spiritual development more accessible and fun in books like:

- *Liberation. The perfect holistic antidote to stress, depression and other unhealthy states of mind*

- *Handbook for the urban warrior. A spiritual survival guild*

- *Manifesto: The internal revolution*

Thanks to Emma and Miss G for your help. Very special thanks to Gail.

Contents

Introduction

I'm an average guy from Essex with an average level of intelligence and like many others I have spent time asking the ultimate question: "what's the point of life?"

At times this question would be asked in a general, inquisitive way and on darker days, it would have been asked in a negative, down trodden and desperate way. In either case, the answers I have subsequently found have created a calmer, more peaceful and happier me and moreover, I can see that my actions can also have a profound effect on the happiness of everyone else too.

The things I discovered on my quest for the answers I have called my *"realisations"*. These realisations are not new and I have not created them myself but they are a collection from various sources. Each of which ultimately answer the question: **"what's the point?"** and opens hearts and minds to the endless possibilities of life.

The discoveries made in the field of quantum physics means that science and religion are no longer two separate entities in conflict with each other and so I have attempted to back up my realisations with a little bit of scientific evidence.

I have written these realisations down in the form of this book merely to help habituate and familiarise my own mind. But perhaps someone else will read these words and as a result, they too will move towards a more fulfilled, exciting and happier life.

By being mindful of these realisations and practicing them each day through the words I say, the thoughts I think and the actions I take, I am creating a much happier existence for myself. I have also found the world around me has become a place of endless possibilities which I am thoroughly enjoying!

I hope whoever reads this also ends up feeling the same way.

Anthony ☺

What's the Point?

What's the point of this book?

The point is to help the reader find a real sense of permanent happiness and contentment in life. Also, to discover new possibilities and become conscious of some very exciting and potentially life changing realisations.

So, if you are prepared to change your life for the better and feel better about yourself, then read on and enter the door to your new and adventurous future. Be warned however, in order for you to discover new lands you may need to overturn a few old stones and cover some unchartered territory. This journey may be challenging for you so rest when weary and then trudge on once again. All journey's start with a single step and the first one can sometimes be the hardest. Likewise the first chapter of this book may start to feel a little uncomfortable but it is necessary. Relax, have an open mind and step forward to explore new and exciting beginnings. Good luck!

To begin this little book of happiness let's start with a real happy statement;

LIFE SUCKS! and then you die!

Let's face it; from the moment we are born we are set on a downward slope of ageing, sickness and finally death. From the moment we are born we are heading towards our own demise.

In the mean time, we attempt to fill our lives with things that we hope will help us become happier and more content. However, all the things we work for, strive for and try to attain for ourselves, ultimately ends up going else where when we die. So, **WHAT'S THE POINT?**

It would seem that we spend all of our days on earth trying to make our lives happier only to find that our happiness never truly lasts. We collect and form attachment to our friends, family and material possessions, but ultimately, it's this attachment that will cause us more unhappiness when we have to leave it all behind and checkout from life. We can't take any of this stuff with us when we die and, in fact, it's the attachment we give to family, friends and material possessions that will cause us more sorrow at our time of death. So, the things we collect and work hard to keep and attain to make our lives happier will cause us more suffering at the end of the day. So, once again, **WHAT'S THE POINT?**

It has been said that searching for happiness in this world can be like drinking salty water to quench our thirst. The more we drink the thirstier we get. The more we search for contentment outside of ourselves and in things, people, places or possessions, the further away from contentment we seem to be.

There are of course some of you who are thinking that this doesn't apply to you because you have everything you could wish for. This is great and I'm pleased for you but I'm afraid to say that this happiness and contentment will not last. Soon, you may find yourself wanting more or something different because you are no longer satisfied. Life is very delicate and you may become ill or lose a loved one, which bursts your bubble of happiness. Unless you are looking in the right place, happiness in this life is only a transient experience. We hear and read about tragic accidents that separate loved ones. We read about the wealthy businessman who has lost everything he owns on the stock market. The truth is that ultimately we spend our entire lives building attachment to our possessions and loved ones only to lose it all through the inevitability of aging, sickness and death.

We only have to look at the rich and famous, who seem to have all the material possessions to be happy, to recognise that even with all the money, relationships and assets in the world, this can not make someone truly content. We frequently read about celebrities who become depressed, have drug and alcohol dependency and even become suicidal.

I can imagine, as a child, a celebrity may have grown up wishing to become famous and attain the glamour of celebrity life. However, once they reach this goal, I can also imagine that their wishes then turn back to their time as an average civilian and they wish to be free from all the increased stresses, worries and hassles that come with celebrity. Being in the limelight can bring more worry about the safety of their family, worry about all the money they have, worry about the prying public eye and of course the hounding press.

In a very similar way, we all tend to look to the future for happiness only to find that it doesn't provided us with true, lasting contentment after all. That's when we look back into our past and wish we'd appreciated what we had. Because we know that the past has been and gone, we turn to the future once again looking for the next thing to make us happy in life.

"Things will be better when…"

"When [such and such] happens, that's when I will be happy"

"If I can just get [this or that], then I can relax and be happy"

This constant wanting and searching causes us emotional sufferings, great confusion and discontentment in life. But lasting happiness is out there for you and this book is aimed at giving you the directions to get you there.

Congratulations!

This realisation is the toughest part. It's a rocky path but now that your eyes have been opened to this cycle of suffering we can begin to move onto easier areas and break our cycle and find lasting happiness for ourselves.

In fact, far from being a depressing chapter, it can help liberate us from the cycle of suffering by helping us to refocus and look for happiness in the correct places by recognising the pointlessness of our material pursuits and misplaced searches.

The Addiction to Feelings

We could say to ourselves that life is a disappointment and that's just how it is. We could reside ourselves to the belief that life's a bit rubbish and that all we are here for is to live the best we can before we die. If that's the way you wish to view your life then that's just fine, but only if it makes you happy. If the belief that we only exist to hang about before we die is true, then why not have a little fun whilst you're here? Make the absolute most of it. Don't waste any time on negative stuff because **WHAT'S THE POINT?** If you are doing something that isn't making you happy, why do it? Similarly, if you are thinking something that isn't making you happy or keeping you stuck in the same negative cycle, why think it?

If you believe that you are only here to make the most out of life before it's all over, then why not do just that, make the most of everyday and change the way you think. Because believe me, if you think life's shit, it will be. If you are here merely to hang about before you die, then surely, life's not naff, but rather a precious, fleeting gift and you are extremely lucky to have the opportunity to make the most of it.

Here's a little example to introduce you to this concept. In a conversation, we may believe that all the words and gestures we are using are the correct ones to produce the desired response in the person we are talking to. i.e. explaining the meaning of life or how to get to the local shop. However, if we don't get the response we wanted from the conversation, we tend to blame the other person. We blame them believing that they didn't understand what we were saying or that they are not listening properly or seeing things from our point of view. This assumption is based on the belief that a conversation between two people is a 50:50 split in responsibility. This view allows each individual to *give up* fifty percent of the responsibility to the other person, thus, when the desired outcome doesn't materialise from the conversation, we can blame the other person because they hold fifty percent of the responsibility.

There's a line in the film War Of The World's where Tom Cruise is playing the role of a father. Trying to convince the characters daughter that he can help her with her homework, he says: *"between me and my brother we know everything, so ask me anything you like"*. So, his daughter asks him what the capital of Australia is to which he replies: *"that's the one my brother knows!"*

This type of 'shared responsibility thinking' takes the control and responsibility away from what we get out of a conversation. If we think this way in other areas of our lives then when we don't quite reach or attain our goals, desires and aspirations in life we believe that it is not due to our own behaviour, but is due to the behaviour of others and events outside of our control. The other fifty percent if you like. This type of thinking puts us on the 'effect' side of life and not the 'cause'. On the effect side of life we have no control and life is something that happens to us. On the other hand, being on the cause side of life puts us in control and we become the master of how we live.

When we move to the cause side and start to understand that each individual is _a hundred percent_ responsible for the response and outcomes in their life, we realise that we are in control, we cause positive things in our lives, we are a hundred percent responsible.

I know you could list a whole bunch of events that you would say were completely out of your control but it's how you choose to view that event and respond to it that makes all the difference. You are one hundred percent responsible for the outcome of the event, no matter how negative it is.

To quote another film: _"get busy living or get busy dying"_ (Shawshank Redemption).

We are one hundred percent responsible for the results and responses we get out of our lives. If we don't get what we want, don't give up in frustration; it's just that you aren't 'communicating' correctly, so change your approach and move towards your goal once again. Not getting what we want is not due to other people but purely down to the way we are behaving. If at first you don't succeed, don't wait for others to change but change your own behaviour and try again. You, and you alone control your life, have fun with it and put yourself on the 'cause' side of life and not the 'effect' side.

Like Billy Connolly says: _"there's no such thing as bad weather, just a bad choice of clothes!"_

Let me explain. It's all about how you frame your thoughts and experiences. Imagine yourself standing in shorts and T-shirt in the snow. In such a situation, it'll only take a few moments before you start thinking that the weather is terrible, miserable and really, really quite chilly. However, get some gloves on, a nice winter coat, hat, thick socks, boots, thermals and scarf (not necessarily in that order of course) and you're off sledging, having fun in the snow, thinking, "this is great, I love this weather."

The change of clothes into more appropriate kit completely changes the way in which you view the weather. A change in the way you think and view things can likewise completely change the way you feel and behave in your life.

I guess what I'm trying to get at here is that you have the power to create your own reality and your reality is completely dependant on your own options, perceptions and thoughts. For example, if you asked two separate people what they thought of the same party they attended, each person would have their own views, their own personal account and feelings on the experience. For one person the party they went to was brilliant and they had a blast. However, ask the same person, on a different night and their experience may be interpreted completely differently due to a change in mood, thoughts, experiences during the day and different feelings that came with it. Same person, same party, completely different results due to state of mind.

The way we think affects the way we feel, and the way we feel then influences our behaviour and experiences. It's a cycle, but what's more, it's a cycle that we can get stuck in or addicted to.

Just like someone becoming addicted to drugs because when they take them their body releases a feel good chemical, all your emotions can be addictive too.

Think about it; emotions are nothing more than a chemical release within the body that make us feel a certain way. Whether the chemical released within us creates a positive feeling or a negative feeling, the fact is that if it is released enough by the same stimuli, our body will expect it, look for it and seek ways to cause it to be released, just like an addiction.

Stress is a common feeling so let's use that as an example. As we grow we are typically exposed to more and more stress. Stress can come in forms of one off events like an accident or bereavement or health crisis. But it is the small things that build up on a day-to-day basis which create most of the stress in our lives because they happen most frequently. Within an average day, we can find thousands of little things that add to our stress levels such as traffic, driving, the kids, money, our jobs and the weather for example. It is these 'little' stressors that cause us the most suffering and yet, it is also these day-to-day stressors that we have most control over in terms of how we think about them.

The feelings of anxiety, butterflies in our stomach, lack of concentration, nervousness and all those other nasty things associated with stress are all due to a chemical release within our body. Heroin happens to boost a user's dopamine levels whilst stress stimulates the release of the hormone cortisol. Whether it's taking heroin, smoking dope, sniffing coke, or having to get the kids dressed and to school on time each morning, there is a chemical response within the body which the body responds to and eventually, if done enough, will expect, and want more of. We can become, unwittingly addicted to our emotions, in the same way as a smoker becomes addicted to nicotine.

You could argue that drugs cause a physical dependency whilst addiction to stress is an emotional dependency; however, the mechanism of becoming addicted is the same. For example, if you are used to being angry and have learnt to deal with most emotionally challenging situations by being angry, then you are already showing physical symptoms of addiction. How many times have you come home from work in a bad mood, 'looking' for a row with your partner? They haven't done anything to cause an argument but you have, consciously or unconsciously looked for something to create an argument. Come on, be honest. Being agitated, having that butterfly, knotted or wound up feeling inside are all examples (in this case) of the physical withdrawal symptoms from the emotion of anger.

Over the years our body learns an internal chemical response to an external event or stimulus. Eventually it will end up expecting that internal feeling and if it doesn't appear, it will send signals back up to the brain to search for what it needs. For example; speaking from my own experience, as a young lad, I used to be a bit of a thinker. I thought about all sorts of things until I concluded that thinking invariably led to me worrying. Worrying about my health, my mortality, my future, my family. If I spent long enough thinking about a topic I would end up worrying about it. In reality, what was happening is that my thought initially caused various feelings and responses in my body, which is fine and dandy. However, over time, I started to pay attention to the worrying thoughts over all others. The worrying thoughts obviously set off a set of emotional responses within my body that in turn made me feel anxious and more worried. This internal response then feeds back to my initial thought process to confirm the fact that I should be worrying and my brain says: *"see, I told you I should be worried, look what I have to worry about now!"*

This confirmation within my mind reinforces the thought process that got me worrying in the first place. Like any rehearsed thought or brain function, the more you practice it, the more likely it will happen again. For myself, I became addicted to worry so much that when I wasn't worried, my body would miss the chemical reaction and say to my brain: "Oi! What's going on? Where's my fix?" and my brain duly responded by producing a thought which caused me to start to worry. This kept me stuck in the same cycle and experiencing the same emotional response to life. In my particular case, I had 'taught' myself to find something to worry about even when I wasn't worried. In effect then, I was worried about not being worried! ***What's the point*** in that crazy behaviour!

However, don't start thinking that I'm the only weirdo here because I guarantee that you are addicted to your own emotions too. Whether it's stress, falling in love, being angry, being depressed, or whatever it may be. Thoughts create feelings and feelings create our view of the world. You create your own reality by the way you think and subsequently feel about things.

Recognising and changing the negative thoughts and feelings you are addicted to is a fundamental start to making your life happier and healthier.

The thoughts that you revisit time and time again are so ingrained, so hard-wired into your brain that they end up controlling your day-to-day view of life and create an internal picture of who you think you are as a person.

Let's take my own behaviour again as an example; A few minor 'bad' things happened to me during my childhood and adolescent years and, subconsciously, these events began to shape my thoughts. I began to think that life was one negative thing after another and that every time something didn't quite go to plan it was because life was a cruel git and didn't like me very much. I was on the 'effect' side of life and the 'cause' was out of my control. In retrospect, I realise that I actually enjoyed feeling this way; I enjoyed feeling like the victim. I enjoyed moaning about all the rubbish things that had happened to me because it was familiar to me and comforting to me. It also created a sympathetic response from other people too and this reinforces my negative behaviour. I was subconsciously addicted to the chemicals produced in my body every time I thought negatively. So, with this frame of mind, I taught myself to actively seek out the negative thoughts just to get the 'hit' of negative feelings that followed. This became my negative cycle, because the more I *thought* negatively, the more I *felt* negative. I didn't feel 'normal' unless I was feeling a little low about life and myself. With such mental dedication spent seeking out all the crap things that occurred in my day to get my chemical fix, I subsequently ignored or negatively twisted all the good things that happened.

With this state of mind, even if I had won the lottery I probably would have searched for a negative reason why it wasn't a monumental bit of good fortune that I deserved.

For me, if nothing negative happened for a while then my body would crave the negative hormones/chemicals and subsequently tell my mind to search its memory stores for some negative experience in my life to create the associated thoughts and feelings. Once again, I created negative feelings through thought because I wasn't feeling negative. The internal dialog would go something like: "Hang on! I'm not worried or feeling negative! Why aren't I feeling negative? There must be something? Lets have a think and a little search of my mind…Arh yes, of course, I can worry about that! Phew! That was close!"

I make light of this because I can now look back at it and see it for what it really is. It's conditioning, a learned response that I had taught to myself. However, negative thoughts can be a very serious addiction, which can generate potentially life-threatening behaviours.

Maybe you can think of a time when your life has been going well but still there's a little niggling feeling within you, which eventually overrides the good feelings. Before long you have started to remember that you haven't quite got everything you want and in fact, although things are going well at the minute, you are still along way away from where you'd like to be. You remember that you have something coming up in the future which will be stressful. You remember that you haven't got the job you really want or the money you deserve and thus, there you are once again, feeling more negative than positive and you forget that life is going well for you.

I wasn't clinically depressed, and I enjoyed my friends and family but I had created an underlying negative tone or 'colour' to my life, which for the most part I didn't even know I had. Unwittingly, I had become an expert in finding every little bit of negativity in my day, to feed my negative addiction.

I'd leave the house in the morning and forget my car key. Innocent mistake though it is, without hesitation and as an instant reflex, I'd make a tutting sound and say: "typical!" as if this minor forgetful action was "typical" of life's joke on me. Forgetting my keys was not a simple act but another example of how life was generally hard work and how I was at its cruel mercy on the effect side of life. I'd drop my mobile phone and say: "typical!" I'd be late for work and say; "typical!". It'd rain when I left the house to go out; "typical!" The traffic lights would turn red; "typical!". I'd forget to get some money out of the bank before trying to pay for something in a shop; "typical!" I'd trip up some stairs and say "typical!" scratch the car; "typical!" lose some work on the computer; "typical!; Typical!; TYPCIAL!". I'd actively notice, and even seek out every single, minute thing that wasn't exactly one hundred percent perfect in my day and I'd view them all as a personal vendetta against me. I'd become a victim of life.

Of course in reality, these types of things happen every single day to most people, all over the world. They were not special to me; they are not a result of life's sick sense of humour but merely examples of the unpredictable nature of life and the nature of humans. That's what makes life exciting isn't it? I had taught myself to focus on those little hurdles of life when most people would not even notice them or pay them a second thought.

Life is mostly unpredictable but how we view the gauntlet makes all the difference between an exciting, challenging and fulfilling life to one full of trepidation and fear.

So now I have learnt to avoid the *"T"* word entirely. When things don't quite go to plan, I just carry on; being mindful of any negative thoughts that creep into my head and calmly ignore them. I re-frame negative thoughts into positive ones or choose to listen to the bright, happy thoughts in my head instead.

When I forget my keys in the morning, (which is most mornings), I chuckle at myself, turn around and go get them. Simple! Not 'typical', not a disaster, not life trying to get at me, it's just… well, just nothing but a simple mishap which is so easily rectifiable that it shouldn't even pop up on my thought radar. If it rains when I leave the house I think; *"good. I don't have to water the garden"* or if I'm feeling particularly hippy, I like to stand there for a second or two and feel the refreshing rain on my face, thankful that it gives us life. I then carry on with my day taking positive feelings with me. When traffic is bad, I remind myself that there is nothing I can do about it so instead of getting frustrated or wound up, I do the opposite and decide to relax, look around, marvel at the wonder of life and enjoy being alive. This reframing is especially important if the traffic hold up is due to an accident. In such situations, you may have been inconvenienced or made to be late for an appointment but there are others who are in a far worse situation in the accident ahead. Use the situation to be thankful for your life and feel compassion for others who are worse off then you. As for forgetting to get money out of the bank, scratching the car, or whatever little mishap happens during the day, I try not to think about it at all. With such small happenings, I just accept them for what they are, and what they are, is nothing more than an insignificant, miniscule inconvenience that happens to people all over the world all of the time. On the grand scheme of life on earth, such small things aren't worth thinking about. I then relax with a deep breath, smile and carry on regardless.

These are some of the things I do. With a little bit of mindfulness towards your own thoughts and subsequent emotions throughout the day, I'm sure you can find similar things to work on and change. Reframe your own negative thought cycles into positive ones because they keep you from feeling happy.

With a change in focus of thought and mindset, the small hiccups and hurdles we meet day-to-day, fade into the background and all the good, fun, lovely, thankful, beautiful, kind, caring, considerate, thoughtful, pleasant, enjoyable and exciting stuff that happens to us every single day has its volume turned up onto FULL BLAST!

Welcome to the cause side of life!

This is not a new or revolutionary concept of course; in fact it's the basis of what psychologists call 'conditioning'.

Way back in the 1890's a Russian called Ivan Pavlov set up an experiment to investigate the behaviour of a dog's natural bodily functions when feeding. Pavlov began by bringing out food for the dog and sure enough the dog dribbled; - of course it was a bit more scientific then that. Pavlov then started ringing a bell every time the food was brought out and once again, as you would expect, the dog dribbled contently at the sight of the food. However, after a while, Pavlov continued to ring the bell but stopped bringing out the food. What Pavlov found was that even though the food was not visible or possible to smell, the dog continued to produce just as much saliva as if the food was presented. This experiment indicated that the dog's brain had made a mental link or association between getting fed and the sound of a bell. The dogs' physical body had learnt to react involuntarily (internal reaction of producing saliva) to the sound of a bell (external stimulus), even though there was no food around to smell, see or taste.

This experiment has been replicated in many different ways, on all sorts of animals, including humans, and all of them show the same thing. Each experiment showed that our brain learns to associate or relate to certain stimuli to cause internal responses. In other words our brain learns to tell our body to react in specific ways due to what we have experienced and what thoughts and feelings we link that experience to.

This type of learning can help explain some of the strange behaviours we humans sometimes do. Psychologists have developed and use a model called *Cognitive Behavioural Therapy* (CBT). I'm simplifying it hugely so I apologise to CBT experts but essentially, this therapy is based entirely around the way we learn or condition ourselves to behave, in certain situations, or when seeing or hearing certain things.

This type of learning goes on in every one of us, and most of the time we don't even know it. Over the years spent interacting with the outside world we have unconsciously collected millions of experiences and each one produced a thought. This thought would then have produced a feeling, which then resulted in behaviour (voluntary and involuntary, or conscious and unconscious), see the food (stimulus), "MMM, FOOD!" (thought), dribble on the chin (behaviour).

Initially, the stimulus–thought–behaviour link would have been dismissed and put to one side in our brain just like any other experience, but, if we experience the stimulus on a regular basis we begin to learn to react and behave in the same way again.

Think of it like this. Imagine an untouched field of grass (our brain) and imagine one person walking through the centre of this field creating a slightly visible path (single experience). When the next person (experience) comes across this field they are more likely to follow the created path (same behaviour or response), thus, making it even more visible and even more likely to be walked again and again (repeated behaviour or response). Like the stimulus–thought–behaviour link within our brain, the more the path is walked the more likely it is to be traversed in the future. I.e. the more we think and act in a certain way, the more likely we are to produce the same behaviour again and again.

If you end up recalling the same thought and feelings repeatedly, you will learn to think, feel and behave in the same way over and over. It is likely that you will eventually start to generalise this feeling to other similar experiences too.

What negative feelings are you addicted to? What thoughts do you regularly seek out to make you feel a certain way? If they are not positive then change them, starting today.

Let us take this knowledge to the extreme to illustrate just how powerful this type of addiction can be.

Let's say a girl nervously enters a room for a job interview. The nervous feelings are caused by chemicals released within her body and are common for most people in such a situation. A little way through the interview process she feels a new set of feelings such as confidence and relaxation. The interview goes well and she gets the job. This is a positive response that reinforces the good feelings associated with the sight of her new boss who interviewed her. Having made the connection between her new boss and these 'feel good' chemicals in her body, she feels confident and good about herself, especially when she sees her boss. However, at the first Christmas party the new employee has a few too many beverages and she finds herself being sick in the toilet. Emerging from the cubicle, barely conscious and barely able to stand, it's quite obvious that she is wasted. Then tragedy strikes and as she attempts to remove the sodden toilet paper from her knees, who should walk into the loos to see her at her worst? Her boss! This unfortunate meeting causes the employees brain release chemicals, which create negative emotions such as embarrassment and shame. These strong feelings create new, negative associations with her boss. Over the next few days she replays and revisits the toilet incident in her mind and thus, recreates all the negative feelings inside. Mentally going over the event means that she teaches her body to release negative chemicals whenever she thinks of, or sees her boss. After a short while, her brain begins to generalise these negative feelings and they start to emerge at the sound of his name, his voice and eventually, these negative feelings are associated with all male voices and men in general. This generalised association of negative feelings towards men has profound effects on her social life and eventually she forgets the original incident that caused these feelings and starts to believe that they are due to a flaw in her personality. She doesn't know why she feels this way and she feels bad about herself. To avoid these negative feelings she stops socialising altogether and becomes sad and lonely. Her view of herself and self-esteem diminishes into depression.

This is obviously an extreme example – although, unfortunately I'm sure some therapists would say that this is not a complete exaggeration – but it illustrates how powerful our thoughts can be, and how we can unwittingly become addicted or caught in a cycle of negativity due to these thoughts and feelings.

We can also see how thoughts and feelings can colour the way we think of ourselves and who we are as a person and individual.

"I am not confident"

"I am shy"

"I am a clumsy person"

Therefore, I want you to start to recognise how powerful your mind can be and realise that you weren't born into this world with self-doubt, low self-esteem, confidence or whatever. Negative beliefs about yourself are merely experiences that you have learnt and mistaken for yourself. You are not who you think you are. Your mind has created an image of yourself based on years of experiences. We will talk a lot more about this later but for now, understand that who you think you are is not who you were born into this world as. You were born free from negativities and you have been moulded by your mind into someone you believe is who you are. It is this false, illusionary self that we shall call your *mind-created-self* because it is a creation of the mind, a fabrication made up of experiences and not who you really are.

We have taught ourselves to attract exactly the thing that we don't want. We attract people and situations that continue to make us feel naff about ourselves. Whether it's a big old capital "NAFF", or a small, niggling "naff"; either way, it's still naff so let's change it!

If they don't make us happy, then let's change *all* the negative thoughts into positive ones, after all it was our mind that created it in the first place, the mind can change it back.

Why not start identifying your own negative thought addictions and choose to think differently. By doing so, you will not only start to feel more positive but also start to view your life in a far brighter light.

This is not easy because most of your thoughts and behaviours will be a habit and therefore mostly unaware of. You may have had some really bad experiences that your mind finds it hard letting go of. You may have deep seated behavioural cycles that are completely subconscious. In these cases you may choose to seek professional support to help you discover what's going on in your mind.

Start by being a little bit more aware of how you feel and what you are thinking and then flip any negative thoughts over on their head to change the negative into a positive. Be mindful, be persistent and be patient.

It takes a very special type of person to just decide to stop thinking and feeling a certain way without some degree of effort so, if you are like me, then you need to be patient and practice changing your thoughts throughout each and every day from here onwards. Replace your negative addiction to release hormones that make you feel great, feel sexy, feel beautiful, likeable, chilled out, relaxed, considerate or just plain good about yourself.

It's worth noting that it takes about 300 repetitions for your nerves and muscles to learn a certain movement, like the correct way to lift a box without hurting your back for example. However, if you learn the movement incorrectly in the first place, then you may need to repeat the correct movement over one thousand five hundred times before your nerves and muscles relearn the movement correctly.

In a very similar way, once we have learned to think in a negative fashion, it will take a lot more time and effort to unlearn it and change it into a positive habit of thought. So once again, be patient, relax and practice regularly.

To change your negative thought cycles into more positive ones you have three options: 1) You can change your thought, which will then affect the feeling you have and then affect your behaviour; 2) you can try and change your feeling, which may make you behave differently and in turn think differently or, 3) you may decide to behave differently which, all going well, should feed back into the cycle in a positive way, making you think more positively and then of course feel differently.

For example; I used to work with people who had suffered a coronary event like a heart attack. Some of these individuals were very worried about getting back to their normal work or hobbies due to their condition. I recall one young lad who had his heart attack whilst playing football. In his mind, he made the association between playing football and his heart attack. He had learned to believe that football caused his heart attack. This thought became generalised so that he believed all exercise or physical activity would cause another heart attack. His mind ignored the facts he previously knew about coronary heart disease, like the fact that he had a very poor diet, drank excessive levels of alcohol and smoked about 60 cigarettes a day. Instead he single-mindedly focused on physical exertion as the main cause of his condition.

This thought led him to avoid any physical activity, and his lifestyle became severely affected, in fact, he did little more than sit in front of the TV all day, every day.

Unwittingly, by not exercising or doing any sort of physical activity, this young man was de-conditioning his body and conversely to what he believed, his inactivity actually *increased* his risk of another heart attack. So, the sedentary lifestyle that he thought would protect him was actually doing the opposite.

This kept him in his negative thought cycle as he became more unfit, his body became inefficient and this resulted in him experiencing chest pain when he did decided to walk to the shops. This of course confirmed all his beliefs about physical activity being dangerous for him and that it was physical activity that caused his heart attack, so he sat down in front of the TV once again.

Just a quick note at this point: Do you see the similarities between our friend who had the incident in the loo with their new boss and our sedentary, anti-exercise friend in this case? In both cases their negative thoughts play out in their life to become true. They believe they are silly/stupid or are going to have a heart attack, and these thoughts create behaviour that reinforces their beliefs. They end up stuck in a negative cycle and their actions lead them to a self-fulfilling prophecy.

THEY HAVE
CREATED THEIR OWN REALITY!

> *"A person who believes he can't probably can't, however,*
> *a person who believes he can, probably can."*

With our heart attack patient the cardiac team worked to help change his beliefs by challenging his thoughts with information, evidence and facts. The real fact is that playing football at the time of his heart attack was a coincidence; he was just as likely to have been sitting, or lying down when it happened. Football and physical exertion did not cause his heart attack and in fact, well-paced, appropriate levels of exercise significantly reduce the risk of heart attack.

This new knowledge allowed his mind to rethink his own beliefs and challenge his misconceptions. This knowledge slightly changed his feelings towards exercise and eventually we ran through a basic exercise routine that he did without any problems. Coupling his new understanding of the benefits of exercise with performing an exercise routine without any issues consequently fed back positive thoughts and thus, changed the way he felt about exercise. Eventually, and with some initial support, this client ended up getting back to playing football and actually felt fitter then he did before his heart attack.

Once again, we can see how negative thoughts can be the driving force towards our own negative behaviour.

It helps therefore to start to identify and attempt to stop any negative thoughts as soon as they appear in your head, and change those thoughts into more positive ones. For example, when rushing about in the morning, feeling stressed and wound up, we should recognise the thoughts that have caused us to feel this way. On recognition we should then stop the thought process and change it by simply saying something like: *"It's ok, it's ok, it's ok. I am now calm, I am now calm, I am now calm"*, and believe what you say too. It can help to practice visualisations. Take your mind back to a time when you were completely relaxed, see what you saw, hear what you heard and create all those positive feelings that you experienced at the time. Deep breathing exercises can also help calm the body and mind and help get some focus back.

If you are continually feeling low, and can't quite identify any thoughts that are making you feel this way, you can repeat affirmations like: *"I am now happy, I am now happy, I am now happy"*. Or you could choose to laugh, which will change your feelings and will then feed positively into the thought cycle and potentially change your view of the world accordingly. You could also choose a behaviour that will make you think happy thoughts or feel happy, perhaps going to see a friend or watching your favourite comedian on DVD.

So start today, how would you like to see the world? How would you like to see yourself? There is nothing that you cannot be if you believe it and the only way to believe it is by starting to think it.

I should mention of course that there are therapists, psychologists and Neuro-Lingusitic practitioners who are skilled to help people reframe and change their thought cycles. So if you're struggling to change the parts that are keeping you stuck in a negative cycle, you may wish to see a professional to help you develop and move forward (see. www.wisemonkeytraining.co.uk).

Do **NOT** use alcohol or drugs to lift you up, these will only cause a false feeling of happiness and then once all the booze and/or narcotics have warn off, you will be left at an even lower physical and emotional level of lousiness. Using synthetic chemicals to change your mood is a slippery slope into an unhealthy addiction. So why not do it naturally and healthily, using your body's own natural chemical supply by creating positive feelings through thought.

The more we counteract negative thoughts by replacing them with positive or happy ones, the more the nice feelings will take preference. This will be your new thought-feeling-behaviour cycle.

To help stop you repeating unhelpful patterns of thought and help change your addiction to a negative one, I am going to refer to a set of eight verses throughout this book.

These verses may not seem much at first but I promise you, if you read and practice their content regularly, it will transform your mind from one that is often discontented, confused and typically unhappy, to one that is more peaceful and more content.

Before reading the verses, I would advise the reader to complete the book first. Each verse will hold new and more profound meanings after the book is read. For this reason I've put these eight verses at the end of this book.

Let go and let the gem shine

The snow goose need not bathe to make itself white. Neither need you do anything but be yourself.

LAO-TSE

To recap then, we were not born into this world with any negativity; in fact, we are all born free from any concept of self, holding no negative feelings towards ourselves at all. In this way we are born like a perfect jewel, nice and clean, shiny and new.

It is our negative experiences that make us feel bad about ourselves and those experiences are relived though our underlying addiction that demands we think and behave in ways that cause the release of hormones that make us feel the same way, over and over again.

The more we think and behave in certain ways, the more we believe this is who we are as an individual. We were not born with this belief; it has been created by our mind through its own thought-feeling-behaviour cycles. This created-self, we will refer to as our mind-created-self.

You are unlikely to see a young child feeling conscious of what other people think of them when they dance or play. Children are free to live and laugh because they have not yet developed a concept of self within their mind. It is only through the creation of their mind-created-self that the child begins to become self-aware and consider how others might view them.

As time passes the child begins to unwittingly gather more experiences, some being positive and some being negative. These experiences feed into their developing mind-created-self until the child begins to believe that they *are* those feelings and their negative experiences are caused by their own imperfections and not the other way round.

Such strong awareness of the mind-created-self triggers certain thoughts and the negative cycle begins.

Ironically, as we grow, feelings of self-consciousness then reinforce the existence of our mind-created-self and our true child-like, carefree self, gradually disappears.

As the years pass, we gather more and more negative baggage and this begins to weigh us down - metaphorically speaking - and so we may begin to feel unhappy about ourselves or wish that we were more like someone else. We begin to feel generally bad about ourselves and accept that we are "faulty" or inadequate in certain ways and the perfect, carefree jewel we were born as becomes smothered in dirt (negative baggage).

In an attempt to change ourselves 'for the better', we cover our dirty jewel in varnish so that we may feel better or attempt to cover up and disguise our 'weaknesses' so that others don't notice our perceived dirt/ faults. The varnish we typically use comes in forms of pride, acting falsely, trying to be like someone else, using clothes or vanity to cover 'ourselves'. Varnish is used in attempts to convince others *and* ourselves that we are the exact opposite of our insecurities i.e. *"I don't feel pretty so I'll cover myself in makeup", "I don't feel loved so I act promiscuously to seek attention"*. Worst still, we may even believe that we are so faulty, and we carry so much negative baggage/dirt, that we can't see any of our Jewel-self and become withdrawn, depressed, or even feel suicidal.

When we think of our own experiences in the past we can probably remember a time when we dismissed or ignored certain comments from other people without feeling insecure or having any impact on ourselves. However, although unaffected by some comments, we are equally as likely to remember feeling deeply offended, angry or self-conscious about other comments. Why is this?

This is due to two things. Firstly, it is the amount of self-cherishing we hold for ourselves, and secondly, it is due to the varnish we have put on ourselves, or more accurately, the perceived lack of varnish which has allowed someone to see through it and perceive our 'imperfections', to see the dirt that we carry.

A throw away comment made by a friend can cause upset and the friend will say; *"What are you getting so upset about? I was only joking!"*. Why did that person get upset with the comments made by their friend? What are the real beliefs, which hides behind their reason for taking offence? Why did this person get upset when another person would take the joke as it was meant?

For example, we may feel completely at ease with the way we look and so jokes and fun made by others towards the way we look, provokes little reaction or upset within us. However, if we are self-consciousness about the way we look our mind-created-self becomes strong when teased by others and instead of laughing with them or thinking little of their comments, we feel and react very differently.

Comments made to one person with no reaction can create a completely different reaction in another person purely due to their mind-created-self and it's created need to hide the perceived dirt it carries.

The dirt that we have collected over our pure jewel-like self is due to years of subtle and direct negative comments, actions and experiences. Positive and negative experiences over the years have created and moulded our mind-created-self and we believe that this is who we are. We believe that we are weak or lack ability in certain areas because our mind-created-self has us believe it to be true.

The history that has affected us most, creates the most dirt and subsequently needs the most varnish. The more conscious we become of our perceived 'imperfections', the more we will try to cover it up. We tend to subconsciously put a lot of effort into covering up our 'weaknesses' or 'imperfection' – after all, our mind-created-self makes sure that we feel compelled to wish we were better then we are and certainly better then anyone else. When someone makes a comment towards our 'weakness', our mind-created-self becomes very conscious which re-enforces our negative beliefs about ourselves. Whether the comment made was purposefully spiteful or merely a flippant remark, it will make us feel like that person has seen through our varnish and our attempts to hide our 'weakness'. If we believe that someone has seen through our varnish and sees our 'imperfections' (or "dirt"), we feel the need to protect ourselves, perhaps use more 'varnish' to attempt to cover up the exposed area. We feel threatened, exposed and vulnerable which is why we may react in ways that seem irrational to other people. In any case we end up slapping on some varnish such as pride, spitefulness, lies, bravado and so on, to ensure that it doesn't fail us again in the future.

We also try and cover our up our 'imperfections' in an attempt to change them or in an effort to make them disappear. Of course, covering up a stain on the carpet with a rug or turning your back on it doesn't mean that it has disappeared, but may mean that we become even more embarrassed and self-conscious when someone sees or mentions it. Similarly, if we attempt to use more and more 'varnish' to cover our 'dirty' bits in the hope that they will change or go away, we will become very disappointed and even very depressed when it doesn't work.

For example, we may feel that we carry so much dirt that we use varnish in the form of creating false personas. We may use a lot of boastful speech and perhaps lie about our achievements and ourselves. We may have so much self-loathing because of our perceived 'dirt' or 'imperfections' that we believe that no one would like us if they got to know our imperfect self. However, despite our best efforts, someone may still act as if they are not fond of us, or they may uncover one of the lies we used as varnish. When our cover is blown, it feels as if the person has seen through our 'varnish' and exposed our 'real', impure, faulty and flawed self. This then reinforces our negative beliefs about ourselves, and our mind-created-self will say things like; *"see, I knew if people saw the real me they wouldn't like me!"*, *"I'm not likable"*; *"I hate myself"*; *"People hate me"* and thus, we subsequently carry even more dirt and use even more varnish in the future. Once again, do you see how the things we desperately try and avoid end up playing out to be our reality?

In extreme, but sadly, all too common examples, if our attempts to cover up our perceived imperfections continually fail us, we begin to run out of options and may become chronically depressed, feel complete despair, become agoraphobic, withdrawn and even feel self-loathing.

How sad that a person who is born care free, perfect and jewel-like can end up seeing themselves as a lump of dirt and a few failing, worn out patches of varnish. Even sadder is the fact that this is all due to a concept within our mind and not really who we are. In fact, as you read on you will discover that the mind-created-self that causes and creates the dirt is a concept of self that doesn't exist. The concept of "I" which we protect so dearly is a figment of the imagination that has been installed into our minds from the day we became a conscious being. We have learnt to believe that "I" am something real, something within me and something that has imperfections. You will discover that this is not true.

I remember being in a restaurant with some friends and after studying the menu the waitress began to take our order. One of my friends asked rather abruptly if he could have vegetables with his order, to which the waitress explained that all meals came with veg. Once again my friend abruptly and aggressively complained that this fact was not stated on the menu. Even when the waitress calmly pointed to the small print at the bottom of the menu that read; "*all meals are accompanied with a selection of vegetables*", my dining companion aggressively complained that the type was too small and it wasn't clear.

To on lookers in the restaurant and certainly to the waitress, my friend probably seemed to be rude, aggressive and even unpleasant or dislikeable. However, when we see things from my friend's point of view we see that his actions were produced by delusions of mind, self-grasping/protecting and the 'baggage' he carried.

My friend didn't feel comfortable eating in a relatively high-class restaurant and did not feel confident in himself in such an environment. When he made the mistake about the vegetables, because of his low self-image, he felt as though the waitress and all others could see through his varnish (pretend confidence) and directly at his lack of confidence in such an environment. As a result his mind-created-self became very strong and he felt a need to protect it with anger and blame. What would have been seen as a minor mistake to others was seen as a real reflection on his insecurities and perceived imperfections and thus, made him feel silly and as if his 'varnish' had failed him. More accurately, his mind-created-self fashioned a need to protect itself, hence, more varnish was used to switch the blame away from his mind-created-self and onto the waitress and whoever typed out the menu. Switching blame away from himself was an attempt to make him feel better and further disguise the lack of confidence in the situation.

Without the negative baggage, lack of confidence and the resulting need to protect the mind-created-self, my friend would have felt no need to feel self conscious and would have simply asked for vegetables in a calm, polite manor and then calmly accepted that he had missed the small print with no fuss and upset to himself or anyone else.

Once again, do you see how the way he acted inadvertently created a situation that confirms his negative beliefs about himself, i.e. *"I'm rubbish in places like this. I don't fit in. I don't feel comfortable here. See, I've made a fool of myself by not spotting the small print. I don't belong here."*

With this in mind we should *never* judge the seemingly inappropriate actions and behaviours of others. Don't forget that by judging someone you are doing exactly what has fed and formed your own mind-created-self.

> *With a determination to accomplish*
> *the highest welfare for all sentient beings,*
> *Who surpass even a wish-granting jewel,*
> *I will learn to hold them supremely dear*

Verse one

Let us take the example of tripping in public. For most people, tripping and falling in full view of strangers causes feelings of embarrassment and maybe foolishness. The only reason you feel embarrassed is because your mind-created-self believes that other people will be thinking *"HA! He just fell in public, what a fool!"* And this assumption makes you feel bad and silly about yourself. In reality however, people may laugh not because they think you're silly or foolish but because their own mind-created-selves are glad that it wasn't them.

When something potentially embarrassing happens to someone I stop myself from laughing (unless they quite clearly find it funny themselves which most likely means that they carry no dirt in this area) and I always say something like: *"I did that only yesterday"* or *"I've seen so many people do exactly the same thing"*. By saying something like this, I am trying to help the person realise that their 'embarrassing' action is not a flaw in their make-up or personality. Tripping in public is normal and everyone has done it at some point in their lives so there's nothing to be embarrassed about, we've all been there. This of course also helps them forget or dismiss any negative thoughts their mind-created-self may be saying and prevents them creating or adding 'dirt' to themselves.

Generally, it will help you and other people if you try and have continuous compassion for others because remember; they are most likely acting negatively due to their own suffering caused by their own mind-created-self.

You should (in most cases) ignore what your mind-created-self is saying and remember: 1) you can never truly know the reasons why someone may say or do negative things towards you or others; and 2) you were born as a perfect jewel and you still are, so don't listen to your mind-created-self, it's only function is to make you believe that you are faulty in some way and thus, it talks utter rubbish.

The truth is that the dirt we carry and the person we think we are underneath the varnish is not who we really are at all. We were not born with this dirt and negative baggage; the dirt is there because of our mind-created-self. We *are not* our mind-created-self. Our mind-created-self is nothing more than a collection of thoughts and memories that we shouldn't even be hanging on to.

It's only when we realise that all the negative feelings and thoughts we have about ourselves is not who we really are but simply unnecessary 'baggage', we can begin to see ourselves as the pure, uncontaminated gems that we came into this world as. By letting go of the baggage we carry, it makes sense that we will feel lighter, energised and we can start to feel free and happy with who we are.

There are times when someone is clearly saying hurtful comments to get at you. In such situations remind yourself that the person attempting to upset you is doing so because of their own mind-created-self. Their spiteful words will be their own source of varnish, which they use to cover their own perceived imperfections. So, if you are feeling affected by the words of others, remember that your offender is suffering and so feel compassion for them. Also remember that the negative feelings their words have caused within you are merely creations of your mind and as such it is ultimately a figment of your imagination.

When we make mistakes, misunderstand things, misinterpret things, make foolish comments or simply trip and fall in public, we should not feel that this is due to a flaw in ourselves but merely just human behaviour. We should therefore laugh at our behaviour or smile and dismiss it immediately. Who cares?! The only person that cares is your mind-created-self because it makes you feel acutely aware of what other people might think of you; saying: *"What a stupid thing to say. They are all going to think you're so stupid now. You are so stupid!"* But once again, WHO CARES?! Your mind-created-self is your nemesis and not you. Your mind-created-self has one role and that's to make you feel bad about yourself, make you doubt yourself and make you forget all the things that make you special.

"Life's an adventure, travel light"

Let go of your negative baggage and be free to enjoy the adventure of life.

This concept of letting go can be put into practice in small but significant ways throughout our daily lives. For example, I was sent an email from a senior work colleague, asking me to complete an assessment form. I read the form through but it didn't make any sense to me.

My mind-created-self felt a need to protect itself and made me doubt myself and feel that I wasn't clever enough to understand the form. It made me think that my insecurities in this area were justified and that it was a personal flaw in my intelligence that would be exposed by this form. Because of the illusions created by my mind-created-self, I had a feeling that I shouldn't say anything, I should save face, hide my perceived lack of brain matter and plough through the form regardless. However, I stopped such thoughts, recognising that it was only my mind-created-self and subsequent baggage that formed such feelings. I realised that I should let go of these thoughts and feelings, wash off this dirt and just be… well, me.

So, I decided to speak to my colleague and simply say; *"I don't get it?"* And guess what? In reply, my colleague chuckled and replied: *"I'm glad you said that, because I didn't understand it either!"* and together we worked through the form successfully.

However, if I hadn't let go and accept myself for who I am and I plundered through the form without understanding it, I am sure it would have been returned to me to be completed again correctly. This would then have reinforced my doubts about my abilities and increased the dirt I carried in this area. In this way you can see how perceived insecurities and the dirt we carry could be subtly reinforced just by its very presence in our consciousness. The varnish would have failed me and I would have inadvertently reinforced the dirt I carried. Unless we let go of the negative baggage we carry we may end up carrying more.

It's only when we 'wash off' and let go of all our 'dirt' that we realise we are all perfect jewels and it's only our mind which make us feel anything but.

Next time you are feeling worried, angry, pressured, nervous, or whatever, ask yourself, why? What is the reason behind my feelings? Is it because of someone else's mind-created-self feeling threaten? Or is it because deep inside, my own mind-created-self is making me feel a need to protect itself because of the negative baggage it makes me carry?

Shutting up the spiteful one: Separation

So, if the mind-created-self causes these disharmonies within us, how do we get rid of it?

Firstly you need to confirm on a regular basis that you are not your mind-created-self. I have named my own mind-created-self referring to it as if I were talking about someone else, someone separate from me.

My mind-created-self is called *'Little Git'* or *'LG'* if I'm feeling a bit 'street'.

If someone is being a particular pain in the neck, LG may liven up within me and start creating negative thoughts about that person. At the first opportunity I usually tell LG to "shut up!" right there and then. I remind myself that the person I'm referring to is just like me in the sense that they are only acting in the best way they know how with the resources they have available to them. I then think and feel the opposite of LG and become calm, kind and compassionate. Once I notice LG in my mind, I put him back in his little box of negativity and cruelty as soon as possible. Much like walking away from a real physical person who is being particularly horrible and nasty, I 'walk' away from LG as soon as he turns up in my mind. LG (my mind-created-self) is my spiritual saboteur; his presence weighs me down and holds me back on the road to happiness. Getting rid of LG will help make me a better person and make other people much happier too.

"Be not the slave of your own past – plunge into the sublime seas, dive deep, and swim far, so you shall come back with self-respect, with new power, with an advanced experience that shall explain and over look the old"

By continually making a separation between your real jewel-like, compassionate self and your negative, spiteful mind-created-self, you will feel more content and you will react more positively towards people. Moreover, you will eventually allow your real self to take back control of your mind and be free to be happy with who you are, because you realise that you are perfect.

Basically, to quieten the mind and help release our true self from our dominating mind-created-self, we simply need to be conscious of the fact that our mind-created-self produces all negative actions and feelings and prevents us from being content with other people and ourselves.

For example: if you are in a meeting at work and there is one person with a habit which annoys you, say, interrupting frequently for example; we should immediately stop and avert hurtful/spiteful thoughts, anger and frustration towards this person. We should practice patience because such emotions and thoughts serve no purpose towards your own or other peoples search for happiness. Such thoughts are only there because our mind-created-self is thinking it is better than this person. The reality is that that person is only acting 'negatively' because of their own mind-created-self, just as your annoyance towards them is a creation from yours. You are the same, the only difference is that you now know better, you now know that this person demands attention because their own mind-created-self believes it's the most important thing and this will cause them much unhappiness. Don't feel annoyed but feel compassion towards them. Not pity, not a feeling of superiority but a feeling of compassion as if it were a reflection of yourself.

Of course, if they interrupt very frequently, it would not mean that we should sit back and let them dominate the meeting but the words which leave our mouth towards them should not be sent with any mal-intent but rather fuelled with kind thoughts and compassion for that person. For example: *"Thank you Dave. You have contributed a great deal to this meeting and I'm grateful that you are here. You have lots of good ideas and I would like to discuss your ideas with you later. I would also like to hear what the others around this table have to say about what you've had to say"*

If they react badly toward what you have said, then be conscious that it is only because their own mind-created-self feels threatened and thus, retaliates and we should act:

> **As if I had found a precious treasure**
> **Very difficult to find.**

> *Verse four*

Another common example of how our mind-created-self causes a negative, unhappy environment for ourselves and others is when we are in a rush and the person driving or walking in front is going too slow. In this situation we create a negative state within ourselves, we may get upset or even angry at the person because they are holding us up. When we start to question our behaviour we realise that it is ludicrous, and a prime example of the mind-created-self at its worst.

Take a moment and think about it this for a second. We are getting annoyed at a completely innocent person whose only crime is not being able to read our mind and realise that we are in a hurry. Their calm, leisurely stroll doesn't suit our need to rush and they are holding *us* up. *US!?* Who made 'us' and *our* mission to rush more important then another person enjoying their travels? The mind-created-self that's who! And anyway, why are we annoyed at this person? Do we really believe that they deliberately set out in the morning just to slow us down? Or are we thinking that they have been sent to slow us down by some dark force? All our mind-created-self knows is that we are in a hurry and because of its selfish nature it views itself as the most important thing on earth. What a strange and irrational thing to get annoyed at someone for don't you think?

Here's another of the verses I talked about at the beginning of this book and I think it sums this concept very accurately:

In all actions, I will learn to search into my own mind,
And as soon as an afflictive emotion arises,
Endangering myself and others,
I will firmly face and avert it.

Verse three

By averting '*afflictive emotions*', '*In all actions*', we will find that work, home and social life become a lot more enjoyable and much less stressful. Once we are in control of our mind-created-self, our true compassionate nature starts to take back the reins and we find ourselves calmer and able to enjoy life more because we are not troubled by harmful emotions.

In this way we are not only practicing patience, spreading kindness and compassion but we inadvertently make our own lives and the lives of those closest to us, a lot more content and pleasant in the process.

From this moment onwards, I ask you to control your own mind-created-self in the knowledge that it is selfish and that it is not you. Relax when it starts to make you feel conscious about yourself in a negative way. If you trip in public, or say something that you think is silly, this is the time to let go and know that you are perfect just the way you are. Dismiss the negative thoughts that your mind-created-self may be constructing in your head, smile in the knowledge that it is not the real you and that you control it, not the other way round.

Shutting up the spiteful one: Meditation

The other very powerful way to quieten that destructive, self-cherishing mind is to meditate.

For most people, meditation conjures up images of humming hippies, floating in some uncomfortable looking crossed legged position. But good news, mediation can be done in many ways, even whilst standing, moving or sitting in a chair.

There are many reasons why some people meditate. For example, some Buddhist and spiritual practitioners will meditate on the eight verses we refer to in this book to help transform the mind. I would *highly* recommend that the reader also contemplates these verses regularly too because they match the aims of this book nicely.

Think of it this way; our brain is filtering around two million bits of information PER SECOND. The brain can't process this amount all at once so it selects about one hundred and thirty four thousand relevant bits. These bits of information are processed and the mind decides on an appropriate thought, which then produces an action. This is happening every second, of every waking moment. Meditation can help the mind filter out the rubbish and deal more efficiently and effectively with what is important thus, also helping to significantly reduce stress and confusion.

The mind never rests. It is constantly churning over thousands of thoughts, words, discussions and images each and every day. The more it chats, the more we listen, and the more we listen, the more it chats. Even in our sleep, thoughts of the day seep into our dreams and we have nightmares, restless nights and are plagued by our relentlessly active mind.

Think of it this way. Imagine driving in a car at a hundred miles per hour, on a motorway, with hundreds of other vehicles zooming in all directions. Whilst we try to navigate our way through the whizzing traffic, our side passenger is tuning the radio in and out so that we are rapidly hearing snippets of radio stations followed by white noise. If this wasn't enough to deal with, you also have a back seat passenger who constantly asks the obligatory question: *"Are we there yet? Are we there yet? Are we there yet?"*

Just like the mass of information that hits our five senses every second of every waking hour, our high speed, noisy and chaotic motorway drive makes us easily distractible, and we find it hard to concentrate, probably becoming highly stressed and very likely to make a disastrous mistake.

This sort of chaotic bombardment of information is what we have become accustomed to in every day of our lives. Our brain is constantly processing and filtering millions of stimuli every second and we can find even the simplest of tasks stressful because of it.

Now imagine that we are on the same motorway but this time everything is peaceful. All the cars have slowed right down and spread out at a safe distance. The radio is switched off, and we have no passengers. This time round we have only the quiet, open road to concentrate on and therefore, in this scenario, our driving would be far more relaxed, precise and efficient, and we are far better equipped to deal with any potential emergency manoeuvre.

Just a few minutes of meditation each day could help achieve this type of inner peace and quiet by *'shutting up the spiteful one'* inside our heads (mind-created-self). Meditation allows our mind to filter out all the rubbish and concentrate on just the things that are important and necessary at any given moment in time.

It's no wonder that regular practitioners of meditation have lower heart rates, lower blood pressure, are less stressed, they sleep better, and feel more content with themselves and their lives. Regular meditators tend to be far more productive and able to deal with day-to-day issues concisely and effectively.

Of course, not only does meditation help re-train the mind to be much less active and chaotic but by regularly focusing the mind on one thing, or better still, focusing on absolutely nothing at all, our mind is clearer and we enjoy the present moment, HERE and NOW (you'll see why this is a good thing as you read on).

There are many ways to meditate and to be honest, there is no set way, but more a matter of what suits the individual. The main priority is to re-train the mind so it thinks less, so that it is calm and quiet. We know the importance of resting every other muscle in our body so why not start including the mind too?

To start with you should try as best as you can to limit as many distractions as possible, like switching off your telephones and any electrical equipment that may distract you and choose a relatively quiet place and time where you are less likely to be disturbed.

You can sit on the floor or a chair as long as your back is straight. To ensure your back is straight, try and imagine a piece of string running from your backside (fixing your bum to whatever it is you are sitting on), through your spine, all the way up your back to the neck, passing in between your ears and out the crown of your head. Imagine now that this string is pulled tight at the top thus, lengthening and lifting your spine allowing all your bones and limbs to simply hang, comfortably, relaxed in a natural position with your shoulders back and head looking forwards.

Once in this position you are ready to start practicing being still in body and mind and attempt to immerse yourself in the tranquillity of the present moment.

There are several ways to do this and again, it's whatever suits you. You can count slowly, concentrating on each number as you say it, you could concentrate on your breathing or simply just, well … be still and try not to think at all.

In any case, you will find that your mind is far from still and it will chatter with questions. There may be noises that distract you or the mind may deliberately try and sabotage your attempts to quieten it by interrupting with thoughts. But be patient, remain calm and persevere.

As an aside note; when you practice this in the initial stages, meditation can be a good way to confirm the fact that your mind is a separate thing from the real you by noticing how the mind chatters away while the real you waits patiently 'underneath'. Much like another person observing someone else talking, the observer is the real you.

Anyway, whatever rubbish your mind brings to your attention whilst trying to meditate, you should immediately and *calmly* let it go and get back to clearing your mind once again. If you're counting, start back at the beginning once again, if you're focusing on your breathing, re-focus, and if you're trying to clear the mind then just observe the thought and calmly, slide it back out of the mind, clearing it once more.

To begin with, it is common to find that your mind seems more active when you meditate. This can be frustrating but practice patience and remember that your mind thinks it's all-important and does not like being pushed aside. Persevere and it will eventually quieten down. Remember you have spent many years believing that you are your mind-created-self so it's only natural to find it may take a while to shut it up.

Also, your mind may seem to get noisier and noisier purely because you are focusing on it. In fact, it's not getting busier but that's how busy it always is, you just haven't noticed before.

Practice your meditative routine daily for at least ten minutes and you will find that your mind quietens and the real you begins to emerge and throughout your day, worries will diminish.

You can of course practice this type of mediation when you are performing quiet chores or hobbies such as ironing, painting, walking, getting dressed, or even eating. Basically, the more you practice clearing the mind and spending some quiet time in the present moment, the easier it becomes and of course eventually it will happen automatically.

There are ways to make your meditative sessions personal and tailored to suit you. For example, if you have a good imagination, then use this trait to focus the mind and stop it chattering.

The Western Taoist Barefoot Doctor describes a really nice and imaginative meditative practice in his book, *The Urban Warrior*, which I shall paraphrase here for your potential interest.

Once you have positioned yourself correctly and prepared yourself for meditation, start to concentrate on your breathing. As the belly rises on inspiration, picture waves at the bottom of a cliff (i.e. the bottom of your spine) receding away before they wash back in as you exhale. Spend time imagining the waves in your belly rolling in and out as you breathe, hear it, see it in your minds eye, smell and feel the spray from the sea breeze.

Imagine the waves are crashing against the back of your spine which you now imagine is the bottom of the cliff and when you are ready, travel up the cliff face, noticing all the nooks and crannies as you do so. Notice the dampening sound of the waves below as you float up. Once again, spend time travelling up this cliff face and experience it through all your imaginary senses. When you reach the area of your heart, you will find a cave and when you venture into this cave you find a Buddha in the meditative lotus position looking completely at peace. Feel the Buddha's' peace within yourself as you watch. Then, once you are filled with calm and fully relaxed like the Buddha, the Buddha will send out a beam of light from his heart, which radiates warm love and compassion through you and bursts out of the cave, out of your chest and fills your internal and external space with joy and compassion.

The Barefoot Doctor continues with this very nice meditative imaginary story up through the spine to the top of the head and before you know it, you have been sitting in a peaceful and calm meditative practice for fifteen minutes, with little or no interruptions from your mind.

However, you may be more of a phonetic or auditory person and sitting in a park meditating on the sound of the wind or by a river, may suit you better. You may wish to use one of the many meditative CDs that are available to buy nowadays. The point is that you should focus the mind on one thing or nothing at all, thus, clearing the mind of all other thoughts so that it learns to be quiet, leaving you to be able to think more clearly, concentrate more effectively and generally feel a lot less stress and much more able to cope.

Meditation can of course also help train the mind to be positive instead of negative. Meditation can be used to help you become more enlightened by focusing on something peaceful, beautiful or spiritual, like a flower, a picturesque landscape or a statue of a Buddha. You can even meditate on the concept of death so that when you rise from your meditation, you enter back into the day with renewed vigour in the knowledge that life is precious and every moment is special.

Meditation is an extremely powerful tool towards the pursuit of happiness and should preferably be practiced for *at least* ten minutes each day.

Setting time aside for ourselves for meditative practice can be hard at first because western culture has conditioned us to feel guilty about taking time out for ourselves. Also, we often think that we just haven't the time because we're 'too busy' and before we know it, we haven't mediated for weeks. So, once you have planned a meditative session into your week, don't change it. If you are too busy, then reframe the thought and recognise that this is exactly the reason why you need to take time out to meditate. Think of it this way, ten minutes spent in meditation could end up giving you many more minutes to yourself during the day due to a more effective and efficient mind.

For most people, our day-to-day schedules change, so first thing in the morning tends to work best for most people and it's a great way to start the day.

Also, don't forget that we typically don't tend to focus on quietening our mind and so when we do, it seems like the mind is busier than ever before. If you recognise this, don't let your mind-created-self make you feel frustrated or annoyed, instead, stop for a second or two, relax yourself once again, take a few deep breaths and calmly start again.

With a little bit of patience and perseverance, meditation will very quickly become an activity that you will look forward to and one that you will notice huge physical, emotional and social benefits from.

Quick recap

We've established that after all these years of thinking we are our mind-created-self, we suddenly realise that we are something separate from it. We are in fact, perfect, kind and compassionate and we should love ourselves dearly for that, if not also for all the other amazing, astounding and fantastic things which make us the unique creation that we are. The only thing that has us believe otherwise is something that has been created by our mind. The real you didn't create it, the mind-created-self was born out of experiences, beliefs, and values, which are all an interpretation of the mind. *You*, the real you, is something special, lurking beneath, smothered by your mind-created-self which has grown to be dominant. The negative beliefs about ourselves are fabrications of the mind and sadden our true self. This is one of the reasons why we are never really satisfied with our lives and we get that niggling feeling that there's something more to it. That 'something' is very special…it's the real you. But there's more….

Literally, no mind

Most of us have been living a lie created by our own minds. Without questioning it we have assumed that the thing within us, that something we call 'me' or 'I', and the thing within our body that is looking, interacting and walking around in this big old world is something real, something solid within us. However, if we stop and attempt to find its whereabouts, we find nothing.

Where is this thing I call "me"? Where is this concept of 'I'?

The concept, the idea and the image you have of yourself is merely something that your mind has created; hence we call it: 'mind-_created_-self'.

This is a tricky concept to understand but one that, if you are able to comprehend it fully, will have massive consequences on the way you view yourself for the better.

I would like you to think of a time in which your concept of self was particularly strong. Like when we have been embarrassed or have been insulted by someone and you became very self-aware.

Think about this and hold onto the concept that 'you' exist in the physical sense that you feel is in your body somewhere. Feeling it? Good. Right then let's find it.

So, if you exist, where are you? You can feel that it's something within you, so are you your mind?

The mere fact that we say "my" mind implies that it is not *us* but something separate from us. The possessor and the possessed cannot be one in the same. Why say "*MY* mind" if the mind is what we are? If we are our mind then we would not use the word "my" as if it's something we own or possess, like "*my* handbag" or "*my* coat". We use the word 'my' because it's something we own, we possess and something that is completely separate from who we are.

Also, don't forget that your mind has several states of consciousness. Your mind has several levels of awareness, like being awake and asleep for example. But even though your mind is in a completely different state when asleep from when you are awake, the real you remains the same. So, you are not your mind that's for sure.

We can say the same for "*my* body". We say: "*my* body" when referring to the collection of digits, limbs, head, blood and all the other bits and bobs that make up our physical vessel. Because we instinctively use the word "my" when talking about our body, we already refer to our body as something separate from who we really are.

So, am I the parts of my body, like the arms, legs, blood, or bones? Once again we refer to these parts as something that we own and something that belongs to us i.e. "*my* leg"; "*my* bones"; "*my* heart" etc.

Am 'I', perhaps a combination of all these things? Shove them all together and bosh! Bob's your uncle, there we are!

Alas, we have established that 'I' am not my mind, my body or its parts so how can 'I' become 'me' just by putting them all together? This would be like having a pot load of veg, such as tomatoes, peppers, courgettes, mushrooms and some garlic, cooking it up in a wok, putting it on a table a declaring: *"Honey, I've cooked us some chicken!"*. The individual veg is not chicken so putting them altogether isn't suddenly going to make it into chicken now is it. Similarly, how can a collection of things that we have established that are not who we are, suddenly become this seemingly physical entity within us just by putting them all together?

If we are not our mind, body, or its parts, then if we take them all away we should find what we are looking for, we should be left with 'I'. Take them all away and we should discover this internal thing we cherish and protect so strongly. Remove them all and we should find the thing we cherish and protect whenever someone calls us hurtful names and the thing that we become very aware of when embarrassed.

So, we are not our mind. Take that away.

We are not our arms, legs, fingers, blood, bone or any part of our body. Take that away too.

So here we are then! Hey presto! ... Absolutely nothing!

We don't exist as we think we do! WE, YOU, ME, EVERYONE has been tricked from an early age into thinking that we are our mind, we exist somewhere within ourselves, within our bodies, perhaps within our mind but in fact, we aren't anywhere to be found.

Scientist call the real you, the "observer". They have tried and tried to find this "observer", but still cannot find anything.

Even at a quantum level, which is a level at the atom and beyond, down to the very essence that makes everything everything, scientists still cannot put their finger on where we exist.

In fact, what they have found is nothing. Well, that's not exactly true, what they find is what the quantum physicists call "wave potential". Wave potential is basically, waves of energy, like waves of light, sound or radio, all of which aren't solid and in fact they don't exist until it 'hits' something. This is why it's known as 'potential' energy. Sound waves for example, are floating around all the time but it's only when one hits our eardrum that we know it's there because its energy is interpreted by our brain as sound. Up until that point however, it didn't exist, it was silent energy waiting to be heard.

We'll talk a lot more about this concept of wave potentials in a later chapter but for now, let's leave that one for the Steven Hawkins of this world because '*my*' brain hurts!

This inability to find this concept of self, demonstrates once again that we are not what think we are, and in fact we are an illusion. Most of us have never questioned who we really are but subconsciously believed that we are somewhere inside us. But we're not! The concept you have of yourself, as this thing somewhere inside you is not there at all. We are protecting something that doesn't exist. This concept has merely been created by our minds over many years and thus, can be referred to as our *mind-created-self* or, because of its selfish nature, some call it the *Ego*.

A young child doesn't worry about what others think of them. They play, dance and laugh in public without any care for what others think. Children do not become embarrassed until their mind has collected enough experiences and observed enough things to begin to create and learn a set of feelings, thoughts, emotions and opinions which separates itself from everyone else. Up until the creation of their mind-created-self they didn't view themselves as separate, they just existed, happy and free to simply exist.

Moreover, what we think is what we feel and what we feel moulds our thoughts. Over the years we have had billions of experiences, all of which created a certain thought and subsequent feeling. The more often we revisit a certain thought, the more we get addicted to the resulting feeling. Eventually, our mind creates a sense of self, based on these thoughts and we believe that we are not confident, or good at relationships, speaking in front of people, or even that we are not likable. Our mind has created a sense of self and we end up believing is who we are.

Some people can become very uncomfortable with this concept, after all, if you do not exist as you think you do, then who are you?

This is ok and we'll come onto who you really are later in this book, but for now, let's just have a look at what this all means to you and your life from here onwards.

You might be the one that grasps this concept right from the start and becomes instantly enlightened (you lucky thing you!) but for the rest of us who may understand it but don't quite know what to do with the information; what does this mean for us and how does this affect our life and happiness?

By understanding that you do not exist as your mind would have you believe allows you to be a little more child-like once again. With this understanding you can begin to realise that all the negative fixations you felt about yourself, all those times that you have embarrassed yourself or cringe at the memory of something 'silly' you once said or did, actually doesn't matter anymore. You can now be who you want to be in the knowledge that you don't exist as your mind would have you believe and thus, you are free. Free to be child-like if you wish! Free to dance without feeling self conscious, free to not worry about what others think of you, free to relax and just be who you were born into to this world as before your mind taught you otherwise.

You will know that any judgement or negative comments made by others, fall effectively on nothing. The only thing that makes you feel bad or even care what others think isn't you, it's the mind-created-self, and that's an illusion! The mind-created-self doesn't exist.

Moreover, those who judge you are trying to affect your mind-created-self so that their own mind-created-self can feel superior. With this in mind, when you meet such people you don't care, you can have fun dancing the night away, singing your heart out or laughing with free abandon because you cannot be affected and you realise that there's nothing to affect.

Good news! This mind-created-self does not exist, it's not real and it's not you, so sticks and stones may well break our bones but words and whatever anyone thinks of you, can truly never hurt you! So, be free to be exactly who you are, because who you are is just fine and I'd even go as far to say that you are gorgeous.

However, you must bear in mind that other people are still trapped by their mind-created-self. If you make immediate and massive changes, and start jumping around like a child all of a sudden just because you can, you may embarrass other people (or get locked up!) so, I'd suggest reining it in just a little bit for the sake of other people or at least until everyone becomes 'awake' in the same way too.

Just like a rainbow we see in the sky is actually not there, our conception of 'I' is also an illusion created by our mind. We see the rainbow as a solid object because that's how our mind interprets it but when we try and find it, we find nothing but emptiness.

When we realise that our mind-created-self is just like the rainbow and nothing more than an illusion, we can be free from suffering. We cannot be affected by life anymore, we have no need to protect and worry about how people view us or negatively affect us because there is nothing to protect or worry about.

We begin to realise that *all* humans are trapped by the same illusion of mind and that this is of utmost significance towards true and lasting happiness.

Other people may insult, argue or try and score points against us because their mind-created-self is feeling threatened or jealous. People act in negative ways due to a trick of the mind that causes them to be upset and directly or indirectly upset others around them.

The amount we suffer is directly proportionate to the amount we grasp at our concept of 'I'. Think of the person who has a strong self-cherishing. It is this person who gets upset when friends affectionately tease them in a fun manor, whereas the person with no self-grasping can laugh with their friends and does not feel compelled to protect themselves with negative emotions.

So, if the continued discontentment in our lives is the illness, and our mind is the cause or diagnosis of this disharmony, the realisation that it's all an illusion and a trick of the mind is surely the cure?

Who are we?

This is the question you now want to know I guess. If you aren't this person that chats away in your head, if this person is merely a creation from the mind, then who are you? We must be something right? Well, yes and … er, no!

I'm going to start heading into an area, which requires a bit more from you and a bit more of an open mind. So prepare yourself, relax, control that mind-created-self of yours and open up.

There are ultimately two aspects to the outside world; there is space and things within space. Our body is just something within space but our true nature, our true being, is the energy force, the consciousness of the space between. I don't mean 'space' as in moon, stars and all that but, in this case, I mean the space between the atoms, molecules, cells and organs that make up our body.

This conscious energy is our true nature and if we tap into it by letting go of all baggage, thought and thus, the concept of our mind-created-self, we discover our true form, the real us, and a whole new world of endless possibilities.

I haven't completely lost the plot, honest! Ask a quantum physicist because they have recently found out something very exciting and astounding.

Quantum physicists are those very clever people that look at the very nature of everything at a level beyond the microscopic. They look at the very building blocks of everything in the universe. They study what makes an atom an atom, what makes an electron an electron or a photon a photon. These things are the minuscule building blocks that make the cells in you, me and everything in between.

These scientists have found that the centre, or nucleus of an atom is made up of smaller particles named neutrons and protons. The scientists then looked deeper still and started to investigate what the neutrons and protons were made of. As they investigated they found that these particles aren't actually solid but more like waves of energy, much like a sound wave or light wave. Waves are not solid, they cannot be seen but we know they exist because of the energy they create when 'hitting' other things.

So, hang on just a minute. Let's have another look at what these scientists have found out. We know that we are made of cells and these cells are made of atoms. Atoms are made of things called neutrons and protons and these are waves of energy. So basically, the thing that makes everything you see and touch are made up of waves of energy. Like our own physical body and its cells, a house is made of bricks, these bricks are made of clay, clay is made of atoms, atoms are made of protons and neutrons and these are made of non-solid waves of energy.

Waves of energy, like sound waves, are not solid and cannot be seen, so, we are not solid either!

You can argue that the table in front of you is solid because you can feel and see it, right? But remember that sight, sound; touch, smell and taste are all interpretations of the mind. All of our senses are electrical connections made by our brain to help us make sense of the world around us.

When a baby is born they don't immediately look at a face and see it as a face but rather they see a kaleidoscope of colours, swirls and forms that eventually their mind will interpret and organise to make sense of. A baby's brain hasn't developed the ability to filter out all non-essential stimuli yet and indeed, a baby's brain hasn't created mind yet to interpret it all. A baby's brain is receiving two million bits of information every second and is frantically trying to make sense of the one hundred and thirty four thousand bits it can cope with.

Over time our brain gradually makes connections, associations and eventually creates a meaningful interpretation and picture of what it is receiving through its senses. So, the reason you see the things around you as solid, is because that's the way your brain has decided to interpret it. A default setting if you like. Some peoples brains don't quite default to the same interpretation. In colour-blind people for example, what you see as blue, they may see as red. Some peoples internal wiring makes them taste, smell or see colours when certain words are said. Their mind has made sensory connections outside of our minds default setting, which, for most of us, are alien and strange, but is completely real to them and how they see and experience the world. Who's to say that their view of reality is not more accurate then our view?

The world that we see looks the way it does because of the way our brain has interpreted the information. However, a mind unconditioned and 'untrained' by this is one that looks at the world completely differently. There's a story about the natives of southern America, which illustrates the interpretation of the mind and how we view the world. It is said that when Columbus sailed onto the shores of South America, the natives could not see the ships because their mind had no way of interpreting the information because it was unlike anything they had experienced. It was only after noticing the unusual behaviour of the waves lapping against the ships hull that their minds eventually formulated an interpretation and allowed them to see the ships directly.

In fact science now suggests that the things we see are indeed not the way our minds would have us believe but in truth, every object in this universe are made of waves of energy and are not solid at all.

If they are not solid, then how can we touch them?

You are not actually touching anything but the energy from the electrons in your hand (which are not solid by the way) are repelled by the energy from the electrons in the object you touch. Just like two south-south facing magnets repelling each other, you never really touch anything but you feel the sensation and your mind interprets that as feeling something solid. You are in fact levitating as you read this.

Now, of course I'm no physicist and certainly not qualified to lead you any further down this very strange road but I can say enough to get your mind to open up a little bit more so that you can understand that what I am saying is not just some idea I've had whilst intoxicated or indeed some fantasy of mine.

Fact: Science has discovered that the fundamental building blocks that make you and every single cell, atom and 'particle' in the universe is not solid but a wave of energy that can not be seen, or pinpointed to one location.

A wave of energy is not solid and in fact is not there in the conventional sense because you can't see it, touch it or feel it. The only way you know its there is because it affects other things around it. Take a sound wave for example; you can't see, touch or feel it but you know it's there because it's energy is interpreted by our mind as sound. The only reason we know that sound waves exist is because when a sound wave hits our ear drum, the energy causes our eardrum to vibrate. That vibration is interpreted by the brain as a sound, but up until that point the sound wave was just floating around as potential energy. It is "potential" energy because it doesn't exist until it hits our cardium.

The cells within you are made up of atoms, those atoms are made up of protons and neutrons and those protons and neutrons are made up of waves of potential energy just like sound waves. You are not solid. The only reason you exist is because you interact with the other waves of energy around you. Up until that point you are nothing but potential energy.

It is only your mind that makes you see yourself and everything around you as solid. In reality however, you, this book, myself and everything are waves of potential energy, all mixed together like a soup waiting to interact and be discovered.

I KNOW what you're thinking but it's true! You and everything you see, touch, feel and taste is made of the same non-entity; the same 'wave potential'.

If that's not utterly amazing in itself, think of the larger implications and recognise that nothing exists as we think it does. In fact the only true nature of all phenomena in the universe is emptiness.

Like a reflection in a mirror, we see the object as something that exists, like a mirage in a desert and the rainbow in the sky, our mind sees them as real, solid objects. In this case the only reason we know the mirror image and rainbow do not truly exist is through science and the knowledge and understanding that comes with that. Similarly, all things around us are seen as our mind has created it to exist but all things are not as we believe them to be and are illusions of the mind. Just like we know the reflection in the mirror not to be real, science now tells us the truth and I believe that eventually we will all see the true nature of everything directly and there will be no separation between any of us or anything around us. This may not happen in our lifetime but as science continues to support these realisations the human race will begin to see all things as they truly are and not as the mind has interpreted it.

This will be a truly enlightened world and I am excited about it.

Once we rid ourselves of our minds illusions, we are able to see the real reality of all things. Buddha's describe this feeling like a bird flying through the sky, with no obstructions or illusions, our minds are free to fly amongst the emptiness and mix freely with all that surrounds us.

I can understand that this may seem like a strange concept but I guess it would be no stranger then attempting to tell a newborn that the reflection they see in the mirror or within the TV does not exist as their mind would have them believe.

To help understand this concept, it may be helpful to understand that all objects around us, which includes ourselves, are more empty space then matter.

"...if an atom were expanded to the size of a cathedral, the nucleus would be about the size of a fly..."

William Cropper, 2002

"...it is still a fairly astounding notion to consider that atoms are mostly empty space, and that the solidity we experience all around us is an illusion .... When you sit in a chair, you are not actually sitting there, but levitating ..."

Bill Bryson: *A short History of Nearly Everything*

What physicists first discovered is that all things are more space then solid matter. Now they have found what they thought was solid, are in fact waves of non solid energy.

Take a ball for example: we see it as something separate from the floor it rests on. Separate from the hand that picks it up and the air that it travels through when we throw it. We see the ball as a solid thing that exists on its own. However, knowing that the ball is actually far more space then solid matter, in reality, the ball is in fact mostly empty space, sitting amongst more empty space. Moreover, even the 'solid' parts of it are nothing but non-solid energy. Conversely, our minds have taught us to see the air around us as empty space, when in reality we know it to be filled with atoms, elements and micro organisms. So, is the truth really so hard to believe that the world we see is not how it truly exists?

Up until this point in your life your mind has made you believe that everything around you is as you see it to be. So, for me to say that it's all been an illusion and everything you see is actually not there, can be a concept that that you may find very hard to accept. So let me try and help your mind get to grips with it.

Think about this statement: *the universe never ends.* At first you may think little of such as statement but when you look deeper, your brain has a hard job accepting it because it goes against everything it knows and everything it has experienced. The road ends. This sentence ends. Your life ends. Everything we know and have experienced has formed the belief that everything must end at some point. So then, what's outside the last star in the universe? If I got in my little rocket ship and set off from the last, lonely, cold planet, sitting on the edge of the universe, when would my journey end? It must end somewhere, at some point and at some time right? No, not necessarily. The only reason we find this concept so hard to conceive is because our brain hasn't experienced anything like it, so it doesn't have a neurological formulation or experience to compare it to. However, at the same time, our brain also accepts that it must go on forever because what other answers are there? Even if our universe is in a bubble, what's outside that, and then, what's outside that too?

In the same way, the reason why you may find it so hard to accept that nothing is solid, and that you and the universe are not separate, is because your brain has spent years having experiences that suggest the exact opposite. However, now that you know that science is proving otherwise, you can begin to accept it and eventually, you may even get to see the emptiness of reality with your own eyes. If you manage to see the emptiness of all things directly, your life will change in ways that only a few would have experienced and it will open endless possibilities for you and all beings.

When you walk down the street, be conscious that you are not separate from the air, you are not cutting *through* the air, but you are in fact *mixing* with it. When you meet and see other people, buildings, clouds, and everything in between, understand that you are not separate but in fact you are one of the same soup of energy, constantly mixing together.

If we and all things are non-solid waves of energy, you are therefore not separate but completely connected. We are one with all things in the universe at all times.

This is perhaps the reason why Buddha's (literally meaning *Awakened ones or Enlightened ones*) are said to be able to go anywhere and be any-thing, at anytime. They are not restricted by the illusions of their mind. Buddha's are able to see everything as connected and having a single source of energy with no separation. Once free from the restrictions of their mind and its illusions, they are able to mix their conscious energy with everything around them. I've heard this being described as being like a bird flying through the sky, with no restrictions, the bird can easily fly wherever and anywhere it chooses.

What's the point to your life? You have the opportunity to be the universe. What better point can there be?!

You are everything and everything is you

For the purpose of continuing to open up your mind to a world of strange possibilities, let's touch on a few more scientific examples.

Electrons are those tiny tiny 'particles' that circle around atoms much like planet earth circles around the sun. Scientists have taken two electrons from the same atom and separated then into two separate containers. They then 'poked' one electron to see what would happen. To their astonishment, the scientist found that both electrons simultaneously moved in the exact same direction, at exactly the same time, even though each were in separate places. The scientists repeated this experiment, moving the two sister electrons to separate tables, labs and even to two different buildings and yet, they found the same thing happening. No matter what the distance between the two electrons, when they moved one, the other moved in exactly the same way, at the exact same time. Somehow the two electrons were connected. Somehow the two electrons 'knew' what the other one was doing, instantaneously and guess what? Electrons are within every one of us.

Physicists call this connection between everything "entanglement" because everything is entangled together as one.

If electrons taken from a single atom are entangled and remain connected to each other regardless of distance, then think about this; every electron and every atom in the universe came from the same singular source at the point of the Big Bang. So, at one point, millions of years ago, the bits that make my body, your body, the grass, water, mountains and universe, were once all bunched together in one place, just like two electrons whizzing around the same atom. We are all made from the same material and we are all entangled together, each and every second of every day.

This has implications on many things like experiences of coincidences, daja vu, sixth senses, intuition, and the potential to get what you wish for in life. But I'll let you think about most of these things by yourself. For the purpose of this book however, I would like you to begin to recognise that you are not solid and you are made up of energy, and this is the same energy that runs through everything and is connected at all times.

This means that I am connected/entangled with you and you are connected/entangled with me. I am entangled with my friends, my neighbour, the bloke who lives down the road; the women and man living round the corner, in the other street, town, city and country. You and I are entangled with everything and everyone.

It is this universal energy that connects us to absolutely everything.

Over your lifetime, your mind has told you that you are separate from everything else around you when in fact the opposite is true. You are everything and everything is you. So next time you look up at the stars, don't see them as something separate and far away, but instead remind yourself that there is no separation from the waves of energy that makes up your body, from the energy that makes the space outside of you and to the star you are looking at. You and that star are one of the same; it's only your mind that makes you see yourself as something separate from it.

Next time you walk past someone, remind yourself that you are not solid and neither is the person you are looking at. The atoms that make you are made of waves of energy and this is the same non-solid energy that creates the other person and everything in between. The perceived separation is only due to the way your mind has learnt to see it.

If you'd like to know more about this sort of stuff then I'd recommend the film; *"What the Bleep?! Down the Rabbit Hole: One movie. Infinite possibilities"* by Revolver entertainment.

The concept that we are not separate is not a new concept. People have been praying to Gods for centuries. By praying together they are directing their conscious energy towards a single source in an attempt to influence others and create seemingly 'divine' occurrences.

Many people put the power of prayer down to Gods actions when it is, in my humble opinion, the power of entanglement that has caused the 'miracle'. The energy and focus put into prayer connects them with the energy of the universe and thus, if done frequently, or by enough people they influence the energy around them to 'call' their wishes into reality. Sounds like fantasy but many thousands of people pray every day, is that not the same?

What I am saying here, and what I truly believe in, is that there are divine influences helping to guide us and those holy beings were once just like you and me. In Christianity for example, the Bible says something along the lines of: *"God is within us all"*. I interpret this to mean that we all have the ability to create better lives for ourselves and every other living being through the knowledge of entanglement and the power of our conscious energy. Perhaps all religious text were written in the knowledge of what we are discovering here in this book, but perhaps it was difficult to explain to the masses or misinterpreted along the years.

Enlightened beings are not restricted by the mind and see the universe as a complete organism in which we are all connected. Therefore, such people have complete freedom to mix and influence all things through their own consciousness.

Jesus, Buddha's, Gandhi, Krishna and other enlightened beings were all humans who liberated themselves from their minds and thus, were free to roam their conscious energy with all things. They were not attached to the physical world so they are with us still because they are all things. They are available to help us when we connect with their energy. This is the power of prayer, meditation and faith.

However, what created or formed this conscious, universal energy in the first place, I shall leave that for your own beliefs or philosophies.

Many people accept other religious or spiritual doctrines without much question but because I am a humble lad from Essex, I feel the need to back up my words with some science.

Professor Dean Radin Ph.D. from Sonoma Sate University (Author of *The Conscious Universe*) found something very profound when he set up an experiment involving a computer program called the Random Number Generator (RNG).

The RNG is a computer program, which produces a completely random sequence of noughts and ones to investigate if it would eventually become organised (Chaos Theory, for those that are interested). The professor monitored the RNG over a period of time and to no surprise found that it was mostly completely random. However, when the attack on the Twin Towers happened on 9.11.2001, the RNG became more organised and a pattern formed. The RNG was no longer random.

Knowing about entanglement and the connection between all things, Professor Dean wondered if it was the collective consciousness of the millions of people throughout the world, focusing on the tragic event that could have influenced the number sequencing.

The professor and his colleagues looked back over the previous months of RNG data and matched its brief bouts of organisation with world events. At the time of these events, the RNG became less random and more sequenced. In fact, the chances of the RNG creating these patterns of ones and zeros by accident or coincidence was calculated as being a chance of one in fifty thousand.

This was statistically significant enough to cause interest and further investigation. The team of scientists took this information a stage further by predicting when the RNG would next become less random. They did this by earmarking specific dates when major events were due to take place and when millions of people would be focusing their consciousness onto a single source (i.e. the event). When the specified date came around, sure enough, the RNG became less and less random and more organised as people directed their attention on the event. Their collective conscious directly influenced the RNG.

If our collective conscious energy can influence the random numbers of a computer, just imagine what we could do for the good of the world if we directed our consciousness towards peace and other positive virtues.

There was another very interesting experiment, which further indicates the power of our collective energy. This experiment was set up to reduce the crime rate in New York City through the power of consciousness alone. A few hundred experienced meditators were called together as they would be able to focus their conscious energy on a single subject without distraction. On the day of the experiment, the meditators projected their conscious energy on the reduction of crime in New York.

The results of this experiment dumfounded the New York police department as they report a huge reduction in crime. In fact, records showed that the only time crime was reported as being so low was when several meters of snow had fallen, physically restricting criminal activities.

This experiment was repeated again in New York and other cities and produced the same positive results.

Imagine what you could get for yourself and all living beings if you truly dedicated your conscious energy to positively influence the things and events around you.

Even without becoming a fully enlightened being, you are able to create many positive comforts in your life and even material possessions, merely by believing that it will happen for you.

With a calm and virtuous heart, your conscious energy is able to send out a 'message' to bring you what you wish for, because you are entangled with all things. This is what some call 'ordering on the cosmos', and now we know about the universal energy that we are, we can see how this works.

So, with a kind and compassionate heart, get ordering for yourself and for others. Keep that mind-created-self under control though, because if you develop doubt, frustration, impatience and subsequent anger, you will be counteracting your positive 'order'. Like any special, or especially large order, the delivery may take time getting to you, so once again, relax and know that it's on its way.

So, What's the point?

The point is that we are energy. Energy cannot be created or destroyed but simply moves from one state to another. You have a unique opportunity as a human being to make the most of your consciousness and become free from mind-created-self, to exist consciously forever for the good of all life today and forever.

In the mean time, order some happiness in your life and ask for double for everyone else while you're at it.

Further problems of the mind

We have spent most of our lives reinforcing the belief that we are our mind-created-self, therefore to think anything different is a concept that we find very hard to acknowledge.

However, if we lie in a quiet room and be still we are able to observe ourselves as something separate from the mind-created-self. Being still in the present moment allows us to recognise that our chattering mind is separate from our consciousness and we experience our mind as if we are over hearing someone else's conversation.

In the present moment we are able to observe the mind-created-self as a separate thing to who we really are. This consciousness which is doing the observing is our true consciousness, the energy, our true self, which is alive in the present moment, in the HERE and NOW.

Our mind lives on thought because thought justifies its existence. It is through thought that the mind-created-self was able to manifest in the first place. It is through thought created by the mind which deludes us to that which is not real or important in life. Thoughts of the mind have us believe that our happiness can be found in the future. It is through thought that we question and seek answers outside of the HERE and

NOW. Our mind produces thoughts and analyses everything around us, asking questions of it and relates everything back to our self.

Questions can act as signposts, pointing us towards the answer to our happiness but ultimately they are not the destination. Thought therefore can prevent us from getting to where we wish to be. Moreover, the more we focus on thought the less progress we make because:

Firstly, it is thought that keeps our mind-created-self alive and thoughts are based on future and past. There are no thoughts found in the present moment because the present moment, right HERE and NOW, is not the past or future. There are absolutely no questions to be asked in the present moment because the NOW is what it is. The NOW is happening right in front of your eyes, how can there be any questions of it that do not involve the past or future?

All questions related to ourselves are set in the past or future: *"if I had what I had 10 years ago then I'd be happy"*. But did we appreciate it when we had it? We didn't appreciate it because our mind-created-self was looking everywhere but the present moment. The mind caused us to miss what we had and miss the life we live by making us spend all of our time living in the future or the past.

There are no questions in the HERE and NOW because the present moment is happening right HERE right NOW. Any questions asked will be in the context of either the past or the future. For example imagine you are sitting in silence, not thinking about anything in particular, just merely sitting and enjoying the stillness. Your body may be still but your mind-created-self is not allowing you to live in the moment because it keeps you constantly occupied with thoughts about what you have coming up in the future or what you did in the past. By keeping you living in the past or future through thought, your mind will prevent you from truly enjoying the moment and will thus, prevent you ever living and experiencing your life which unfolds in front of you, right HERE and NOW.

The NOW has no questions, no worries, no stresses and only peace and contentment.

Secondly, and above all, the past and future are illusions; both past and future take place in the present moment, the HERE and NOW is where it all takes place. Remember the saying: *"tomorrow never comes?"*. Tomorrow never comes because it does not exist until it becomes today.

How can questions, sought in places that don't exist ever be answered?

Plan and be aware of the future, but don't live in it. The past has gone and no longer exists so don't live there either. Realise that everything takes place in the present moment and therefore, the HERE and NOW is where your life takes place. Enjoy it, soak it up, and spend time in it by relinquishing thought because the present moment is your life.

The present moment

Let's say that we did manage to change our environments to meet all our wants and needs: we manage to secure all the money we need, we have the relationship we want and we lived in the house and area of our dreams, would we then be happy? Perhaps for a short while but our mind-created-self lives in the past and future and therefore, it will always have questions, anticipation, wants and needs that can never be fulfilled. The mind-created-self can never be truly satisfied because it seeks happiness in the future, which will never come around.

Surrender to the present moment, don't worry about what tomorrow will bring because this will prevent you from living your life, which is taking place today.

It is good to have an end to journey towards, but it is the journey that matters in the end.

Ursula Le Guin
The Left Hand of Darkness

Surrender to the present moment and remember that peace, happiness and contentment is already within us. By searching anywhere else for it will not work. Therefore, stop searching and start living each moment and appreciating every day, hour and minute. Try not to think at all about what might be, just accept today with a smile because tomorrow never comes, it just becomes today once again. Sure, it is wise to plan for the future but once you have set your plan, forget about it and return as soon as possible to live your life in the present moment.

Also, remember that you are connected to everything; you are the same empty, wave of energy as everything else in the universe. You are also, connected to absolutely everything in the universe. Right now, as you read this, the energy that created the atoms of this page is the same energy that is running the air between the page and that which is your real self. The same energy runs through every atom in your body and every atom in the universe and nothing separates you from it all. You are everything and everything is you. Strange but true… And that rhymes!

Didn't Jesus say: "*The Kingdom of Heaven is within you*". Wasn't he a bright lad to work it out all those years ago? The founder, conqueror Buddha, Buddha Shakyamuni, also knew that we are not our mind and we are not solid but the same connected energy. Buddha Shakyamuni spent 6 years in deep meditation to rid himself of his mind-created-self and eventually set free his true self and connect with everything in the universe.

Someone who is able to free themselves from their mind is truly enlightened and at that point will be able to mix with the universal energy that is everywhere and thus, be anything and everything.

How amazing would that be? The potential to do good for all other living beings would be limitless because you would no longer be attached to the physical world and be able to influence all things.

Non-permanence
of everything

The fact that nothing is permanent in this world also causes us suffering because we attach ourselves to things because we see it as ours and that they will be around forever.

Depressing though it may seem at first, but the fact that nothing physical lasts in this world and that all our wealth, possessions and loved ones will not be able to save us from death, is actually a liberating concept.

Once we realise that all material gains in this life cannot be taken with us when we die and that ultimately the gift of life is extremely fragile, we become free from the falsities of life. We realise that the only thing that is precious in this world is the single moment in time happening right NOW and that love and compassion is happiness.

How's that nice little saying go again?

> *"Yesterday is history, tomorrow's a mystery but today*
> *is a gift and that's why we call it the present!"*

Our mind creates thoughts about moments past and moments to come but it never resides in the present moment because at that point, it can not exist and is destroyed. Our mind-created-self has no function or existence in the present moment.

Living in the past or future often makes us unhappy, want what we haven't got and then want something else when we've got it.

Look back at your own life and think of all the things that you wanted for yourself and recognise how many of these wishes have come true. I bet you'll find that most have come to fruition, it's just that you have been too busy looking elsewhere to realise that you have got what you asked for. If you haven't, then this is only because it's yet to come or you have changed your wishes to something else before your original wish had time to be manifested for you.

The fact that your mind-created-self never allows you to live in the present moment means that you are constantly missing all the things you have gained for yourself.

Our mind cannot survive in the present moment and thus, once again, it causes us to be discontented with life. We think that life never plays out how we would like it too, but if you stop and look back, you'll see that most of your desirers have come true but you missed it by focusing on the next thing in the future.

Yet again, our mind grasps at something that doesn't exist.

Analysing it, we realise that when we experienced those events in the past they all took place in the present moment. The Romans didn't live in the past, they lived in the NOW. When they were walking around building their roads, it was the present moment, the past is just a present moment that has been and gone and as such, the past does not exist. Similarly, the future is nothing but a potential moment waiting to happen but until then, it doesn't exist. So, **What's the point** in wanting or waiting for something that doesn't exist to bring you happiness, contentment and/or peace- of -mind?

Live, love and laugh today!

For example; when the anticipated weekend or bank holiday comes round it will be happening in the NOW. When we jump on a plane for that well deserved holiday, it will be happening in the NOW, on a single day and moment in time. However, the point is, up until you got on the plane you may have been thinking; *"I can't wait to get on that plane"* but when the time comes and you are seated on the jet, will you be soaking up the moment that you have been so desperately waiting for? No, of course not. Your mind-created-self will be ignoring the moment and thinking about getting off the plane and getting to the resort or the bar or beach. You may even be wishing the flight away to get to another activity when it lands and you have completely forgotten that a few moments before, you were wishing to be where you are now. This continues until eventually, you have wished your holiday away and it rapidly comes to the end when you will be thinking something like, *"I wish I had more time. This holiday's gone far too quickly!"* Now you are missing the last few moments of your holiday by thinking of the disappointing reality of returning to work and home life once again.

This example of a holiday is typical of every day controlled by our mind-created-self. Everyday is never truly experienced because it is wished away to the next thing, the next thing, and the next thing. Ironically, all the things we wish for in our lives (mostly) come true but we never feel like they do because we don't notice them when they arrived. We're too busy wishing, waiting and wanting the next thing. We live in the future, and the future doesn't exit until it becomes today.

No wonder our lives seem to fly by the older we get. We're wishing it all away, as our mind-created-self gets stronger and more dominant with the years.

It is our mind that keeps us living in the past and the future, neither of which actually exist. The life we live happens in the present moment, right HERE, right NOW.

By letting our true existence pass right under our noses without even knowing it is keeping us from enjoying and appreciating every living moment and that our time here on earth is fleeting and precious.

In the Bible it eludes to this concept:

> *"You tell man to return back to dust [die before you die*]. A 1000 years to you are like one day, they are like yesterday, already gone, like a short hour in the night. You carry us away like a flood; we last no longer than a dream. We are like weeds that sprout in the morning, then dry up and die in the evening.... teach us how short life is so that we may become wise".*

The Bible: Psalms

It is said that a man once asked Jesus what the most amazing thing about the Kingdom of Heaven is, and Jesus replied: *"There is no time"*. If there is no time, then each and every moment would be truly lived because our mind-created-self cannot exist to keep us from it. Could it be that what Jesus was getting at is that heaven is 'NOWHERE' or rather *'NOW HERE!'*

Furthermore, the fact that our mind and thus, our mind-created-self only lives in the past and future, causes us suffering for another reason.

Our mind-created-self thinks that the future is where happiness is. The mind understands that all opportunities to be happy have been missed in the past because that moment has passed us by and thus, cannot be influenced. So our mind relies on the future to provide the happiness we seek.

"When I have that new job, then I'll be happy"; "When I have that holiday, then I'll be happy"; "When I move house, then I'll be happy"; "When I retire, then I'll be happy".

The things that our mind-created-self seeks in the future are thought to provide our life story with a happy conclusion; our mind says: *"the past has not worked out for me because I am not entirely satisfied or happy, so the future must be where my happiness lies. I shall search there for it"*. Thus, we wish the present moment away to get to the future. However, as we have already discussed, the satisfactory conclusion to our life's quest to be happy will never be found because as long as the mind-created-self exists, it will never allow us to live in the bliss that is the HERE and NOW. Why? Because our mind-created-self never goes there.

There's also a deeper paradox with this concept too. The mind-created-self rushes towards the future in search of happiness but we also know that death awaits us in the future. We know that by wishing time away in the pursuit of happiness we are also running towards our own death. This paradox causes complete disharmony within us and once again causes the mind-created-self to ask more and more questions about what it is that will make us happy. We might say: *"life is passing me by and I still haven't found happiness, I've sought this and that but have never found lasting happiness. I must be quick or most of my life will have passed before I find it. Where in the future shall I look next for it?"*

The sad thing is that we will spend the rest of our lives searching for lasting happiness unless we recognise the fundamental mistake that is; my mind-created-self is not me and in fact does not exist. My mind-created-self can never find happiness because it searches in external things that will not last and in a place, which doesn't exist (i.e. the future).

* *'Die before you die'* is a statement that helps us remember that life is delicate and we could die at any moment and therefore we should act as if we were already dying. If you were given two weeks to live, what would become important to you then? Your life is delicate so 'die before you die' and be free to live each day as if it were your last. Do not get hung up on unimportant worries, do not live for tomorrow. Live and love as much as you can whilst you are still here.

The constant of NOW

"When you search for a wise mans treasure, you know you'll find it beneath your feet"

OASIS (Natures Law)

Once upon a time there was a beggar. Day-in, day-out, week after week, month after month and year upon year the beggar sat on his little box by the side of the road, waiting for people to pass so that he could ask them for money to enable him to get what he wanted for himself.

One day a wise man was passing by and the beggar duly asked him for money. Ignoring the beggars' request for cash the wise man asked the beggar what he had within the box he was sitting on.

With a hint a frustration the beggar replied, "sir, I have no interest in the box when I have no food on my table. It is money I require to get the things I need"

The wise man asked the beggar to stand and look inside the box. After a few more requests and some calm persuasion from the wise man, the beggar stood in frustration at the seemingly time wasting requests of the wise man and opened the box. Inside, the beggar found all the treasures he would ever need.

Like the beggar, the vast majority of us seek the answers to what we think we need, in all the wrong places and as discussed, this is due to the mind-created-self and its reliance on the future. The fact is that we are already in the place where happiness and our entire spiritual needs can be met.

This moment right NOW is seen by our mind as fleeting because of the physical form it comes in. Our mind sees life as things that have happened and things that are to come. Like a conveyer belt, our mind views life as things that come from the future, briefly meet us in the present moment and then rapidly disappear into the past. To our mind the present moment is seen as something where the future and the past fleetingly meet. Thus, our mind has trouble understanding exactly how to live in the HERE and NOW because it believes that it is something that rapidly passes us by. We therefore spend our entire life waiting for the future to arrive only to watch it become history within a second, thus, we never live truly. For this reason our mind cannot understand that the NOW is *not* a transitory moment but a constant *"treasure beneath our feet"* or a box of gifts that we sit on but never open.

Our mind sees life like a conveyor belt that delivers a whole plethora of different experience to us from the future, and then carries them away into our past. However, in reality of course our mind has got it wrong yet again. If you think about it, where does an experience really come from? A moment or a second that brings a different experience in your life does not *"come"* from the future, as if it were something waiting to happen right next to you. Time is a concept created by man and his mind, a second that we haven't experienced is not a "second" at all. It doesn't exist. It's not something waiting to happen or something on its way to us like a moving conveyor belt, life takes place in the present and is not a "moment" passing you by, but a constant, seamless continuation of life that is taking place right in front of our eyes.

The past is just a collection of memories and therefore no longer exists, and the future is a collection of things that are yet to exist. Therefore, neither the past nor the future exists. The future is only a concept in our mind, a concept of time that is yet to take place. It is nothing but a potential experience that we may or may not have. It does not exist. The only true, constant existence is the present, which is happening right HERE and right NOW.

Because our mind lives in the future and past, it has trouble understanding that the individual moments of our day are not 'moments' but an underlying constant. It may therefore, help to explain it further with a little analogy.

Let's imagine that you are an actor in a play at a theatre. You're back stage, constantly thinking of the next scene, getting ready for your next part, thinking about your next line soon to take place in the future. There may be parts of the play that you enjoy and are looking forward to, and there might be parts that you are feeling apprehensive about. In either case, you are constantly preparing yourself for the next scene and once that scene has been and gone, you may briefly look back to evaluate your performance before you once again focus on your next scene coming up in the future. Whilst you dash about behind the curtain the audience are completely relaxed and enjoying the show. The audience aren't thinking of what might be coming up, or what just happened; this audience is just sitting, watching and enjoying the play as it unfolds in front of their eyes.

Our life is the play itself, and our mind is the actor on the stage, running around, constantly living in the future and past by reflecting and waiting on the scenes. To be happy in life we should join the audience and step off the stage, stop worrying, wishing or waiting for the future and sit back and enjoy the show.

Start to imagine that you and your life is a movie. You have an idea of the type of film you have chosen to see (i.e. comedy, horror or feel-good flick) and you therefore have some idea of what direction the plot is going to head in but you do not dwell on it but merely sit back and enjoy the excitement, the thrill and anticipation of it all. Watch your life in the calm realisation that you have chosen what type it will play out to be. In other words, if you would like to live a happy life, full of love and laughter, then sit back and enjoy the movie in the knowledge and expectation of what's to come. Like the film you have chosen to go and see at the cinema, in your mind you are always aware that the overall outcome to your life will be as you expect it to be. Like a film, your life may have some ups and downs within it but the overall experience is what you expected from it, i.e. a love story, a comedy or a horror. How a film, or your life, gets you to that end result is not a concern of yours, you're just enjoying the experience as it takes place in front of you.

Don't try and plan your life out by living and looking into the future all the time, there's no point because the script for those parts of your film don't exist yet. Decide what type of life you would like for yourself and know that whatever subplots or integrated themes are played out, (i.e. sad or happy scenes) be constantly aware that your life is the most exciting and thrilling movie you will ever watch.

Once we step off the stage, stop living in the future and past and enjoy life as a member of the audience and not as the manic actor on the stage, we become still within the moment and enjoy watching life unfold as if watching an exciting play.

It is important not to confuse sitting back and enjoying your life with stepping out of life and society altogether. Using our analogy once again, we can still be in the audience and enjoying the show whilst having some idea of where the plot is heading. In the same way, we can live in the NOW and still have some wish for where our life is heading and behave accordingly. Like having a choice of what movie we go to see at the cinema, we have a choice of what life we would like to experience. For example, if I believe that my life is nothing but struggles and strife, then this is the life I will experience. If I have chosen a life which is full of love, laughter and comedy moments, despite any tragic subplots that may arise, I will experience a happy and fun life overall.

I'm sure many of you will have questions about this concept. Your mind may scan back to the past and look into the future and see some point of sorrow or ongoing life saga which is causing you suffering and you will say: *"how can that not matter?"* *"How can my sufferings suddenly become insignificant in the present moment?"* *"How can I sit back and think that this is a happy life?"*

Like any gripping movie, life will throw some curve balls and yet you are alive, living and you have the potential to view it however you please. Your life is a movie containing all the most exciting, gripping, happy, sad, funny, tearful and most outstanding plots ever. And the best part of it is that it isn't over yet, enjoy it.

What I'm saying is that it doesn't hurt to step off the stage, stop worrying about what the end may bring but instead relax and start watching the show in the knowledge that you are a part of life and life is something special. Be happy to be involved in it, happy to be a part of the experience and excited about the whole wondrous spectacle of it all. Even if certain scenes in your life are sad ones, know that there will be tons of incredible ones to follow. Be excited about it. **We shouldn't even be here!**

The mere fact that we are here at all should help us realise that we are miracles of life and each moment we live is exactly that, a miracle to be thankful for.

We were born from the fusion of two productions from our mummy and daddy (err!). Each sperm and egg were smaller than a pinhead, yet here we are, talking, walking, and learning. We possess a brain that far exceeds the capacity of the most powerful computer known to man. We can filter and then interpret millions of bits of information every second and react to it all within a fraction of that time.

We are miracles of creations made from the meeting of two tiny cells. The two cells reproduce to form four; four become eight and so on. Each cell is given an assignment, a job to do, for which it is given special features. These cells move around to somehow find and pair up with other likewise cells. Once they match up they start to line up in a very specific manner and begin to form the extremely complex tissues, organs and fluid that form our physical body.

The complexity of our own existence is mind blowing and if anything is a miracle, we are.

In our galaxy there are estimated to be a staggering four hundred thousand stars for every grain of sand on planet earth. Yet we have found no other intelligent life forms or at least not been contacted by them.

Scientists say that if our planet took only a small deviation from its position, trajectory or spin speed, then life could not exist as we know it. We would not be here, and you certainly would not be reading this. In fact the chances of a planet like ours having all the necessary conditions to support life are odds of many millions to one, and on paper would be deemed impossible.

Yet here we are. We breathe, enjoy food, company, the sunshine, and our family and loved ones.

So why don't we see our lives and ourselves as the miracle? This is because of the way you think and that's all.

If you spent every morning from here onwards looking in the mirror and saying something like: *"I am alive. I am amazing. I am perfect. I am very fortunate, how lucky am I!"* then you will gradually condition your mind to think more positively about yourself and your life. Through such simple affirmations you can change the way you feel about yourself and your life and ultimately, you will change the way you behave and see your life.

We should wake each and every morning and marvel at our existence and rejoice in every living moment.

Afloat on the same boat

We now know that we are not our mind, and we are not our mind-created-self. We have also discovered that we are everything, and we are all irreversibly connected. There is no separation between the conscious energy that is the real you lurking beneath your mind, and that which forms the moon, stars and sky. How amazing and cool are you!

However, we are also connected because we are all tricked by our mind (hopefully you are a little less tricked by its illusions at this point) and this means that we are all suffering in the same way for the same reason; i.e. our mind-created-self.

It is our mind-created-self that has us view ourselves as separate from others; it is the mind-created-self that makes us see everything in the universe in terms of 'me' and 'them' rather than the truth, which is that you are everything and everything is you.

However, we are also all the same in the sense that we are slaves to our mind-created-self.

By understanding that all our discontentment, anger, jealousy, greed and hate are due to the illusion and subsequent delusions of our mind-created-self, we should start to feel compassion for all humans because they are suffering needlessly for the same reason.

Our concept of 'this' and 'that' or 'me' and 'them', is purely dependant upon our viewpoint. If we practice descending the 'mountain' of mind-created-self and ascend the 'mountain' of other people, we will not only see things from the perspective of others and understand the delusions that produce their negative actions, but we are also able to see our own inappropriate actions too.

Through practice, we realise that if we continue to put ourselves above everyone else, it is like recognising that all our fingers are the same and yet, choosing to save just one (me) and sacrifice all other nine (other people).

Once we realise that we are no different to anyone else, and that all negative and afflictive actions are created on the basis of the illusion of mind, we can meet even the most distasteful people and realise that their words and actions are a reflection of their suffering. When you see a person in rage for example, descend from yourself and recognise the suffering that that person is experiencing due to the delusions of their mind. Understand that this angry person will continue to suffer needlessly and will never find true happiness due to something that doesn't exist, i.e. their mind-created-self. Feel compassion for them and create a sincere wish for them to be free from their mind because their behaviour is a reflection of yourself and all your loved ones.

We are all suffering from the delusions caused by our self-grasping minds and, although one life is important of course, when asked which is more important; one life or nine lives, we would agree to save nine. In the same way, if we appreciate that all negative actions come from the mind-created-self, we start to feel true, lasting love and compassion for all living things, including ourselves.

Whenever I associate with others, I will learn
to think of myself as the lowest among all,
And respectfully hold others as being supreme,
From the depth of my heart.

Verse two

This verse is not designed to make us feel worthless but rather to help us consider the suffering of others whenever we are out socialising or in general day-to-day contact so that we may feel compassion for other people and in turn, reduce the amount we grasp at our own mind-created-self.

Just imagine a world where no one is suffering from the delusions caused by our mind-created-self. No one would get angry, there would be no war and no theft. People would not fuel their sorrows or escape from their lives through drink or drugs. A world free from self-cherishing and self-grasping would be a world free from chaos and one full of calm and loving people.

I discussed this concept with a friend of mine. She argued that life would be very dull and boring if we didn't have the odd argument here and there, or the odd upset every now and then. My friend believed that that's what made life interesting. I thought about this and concluded that if arguing, anger, and upset is what makes someone happy in life and creates happiness within them AND those around them, then sobeit. But if it doesn't produce happiness for all involved then, ... well, **what's the point?**

Like we discussed at the beginning of this book, I would say that a person does not find being angry, aggressive or argumentative enjoyable but rather they have conditioned themselves to become addicted to the negative hormone/ chemical that produce these negative emotions. We all feel comfortable in familiar surroundings and this is true for our internal surrounds too. What we know best and experience most frequently becomes comfortable for us, even if it is a negative state. Does it make you and others happy though?

Put it this way; think of a time when you have been completely content with life; perhaps on holiday, chilling out on the beach, your tunes are playing on your MP3, the sun is shining and at that moment in time you haven't a care in the world. You are feeling completely relaxed and with love for your life in your heart. Now think of a time when you are late for work, your kids are driving you crazy, or you have had an argument with your partner and you are feeling angry, wound up, frustrated and generally ticked off.

<u>Which feeling would you prefer to access the majority of the time for the rest of your life? Which feeling would you rather be addicted to? Which feeling would you wish for yourself and other people? Do you think that the latter states are what makes life enjoyable and exciting?</u>

If I didn't have a negative feeling in my body for the rest of my life then I can honestly say it wouldn't make life less exciting but the opposite in fact. Life is very exciting <u>*in spite*</u> of the emotional turmoil that may arise within us and <u>*not because of it*</u>. I'd much rather enjoy the adventure of life in a world of loving, happy and kind people, then people who fight, argue, steal and create wars with each other. I don't think we need that sort of emotional distress to find life fun and exciting and I certainly don't think it will make any of us happy.

The true life we completely miss

The only true life we have is in this moment right HERE, right NOW.

We now realise that we are all suffering and that everyone's anguish has the same rootcause because we grasp at our concept of 'I', our Ego, our mind-created-self.

We can also see that by giving out a bit of compassion and taking on the suffering of others, we can help create happier lives for all involved in our life.

Furthermore, by viewing others as more important than ourselves, our own self-grasping minds will gradually diminish and we will not only be free from the emotional sufferings of life but moreover, we will actually view suffering as a means to happiness.

Let me give you an example; when we are struggling financially, we should use that time to consider the millions of others who have far less and feel compassion for them. We should also remember that possessions will keep our mind-created-self attached to the physical world and cause us more suffering. When we deal with distasteful people, it should remind us that that person and millions of others are suffering due to their mind-created-selves. Which, don't forget, is an illusion.

The 'life sorrows' we experience can help us dispel our own self-grasping and destroy pride, shunt evil, help develop compassion and create virtuous actions. All of which will ironically manifest a more peaceful, loving and happier life for ourselves.

Let's pick out another couple of verses for you to think about in this context:

I will cherish beings of bad nature,
And those oppressed by strong negativities and sufferings,
As if I had found a precious treasure
Very difficult to find.

Verse four

When others, out of jealousy, treat me badly
With abuse, slander and so on,
I will learn to take all loss
And offer the victory to them.

Verse five

I really like these two verses. I think they not only capture the concept of diminishing self-cherishing through the understanding of the true cause behind people *'oppressed by strong negativities and sufferings'*, but the verses also teaches us to be compassionate of others for this very reason. After all, we can now identify that their negativities are delusions of mind and this will only cause them and other people more upset and to become less happy with life. These verses teach us that the negative actions of other people (even if it is aimed towards ourselves) should help us confirm the fact that we are slaves to our mind-created-self and we should help to take away their suffering by accepting defeat and not retaliate with violence or harmful speech.

'learn to take all loss
And offer the victory to them'.

Through such actions, a person acting very badly towards us can be seen as our spiritual guide or *'As if I had found a precious treasure, Very difficult to find'* because they remind us of how we are all suffering due to delusions of mind and we should form feelings of compassion for all beings.

I love a good debate about these things and another friend of mine came up with a point, which I feel I should raise. My friends point was that if we are feeling compassion for someone, then are we viewing that person in pity and as such, aren't we also viewing ourselves as better or superior to that person? Good question but this is a misinterpretation.

We should not pity someone who acts upon the illusions of their mind-created-self but instead we should have a real understanding, have patience, and feel compassion and a desire for them to be free from it so they can be happier.

For example: if someone robbed my home and stole my goods, I should feel compassion for them because I know that they must be suffering to have done it in the first place. I also understand that what they have taken from me is just material possessions are thus, unimportant on the grand scale of life. I also remind myself that Karma will take from them what they have taken from others and thus, they will continue to suffer. I recognise that the thief has strong attachment to the material world and will therefore covet things that are meaningless at the end of life.

There may be a part of me that covets my lost possessions too, but it is such feelings that caused the thief to steal from me in the first place. I should not hold onto such thoughts and recognise how we are both suffering from our mind-created-self. I should feel compassion for the person who took my goods because I know they are suffering for the same reasons that cause me to grasp at the goods they took. I feel sad and compassionate towards them in the knowledge that they are causing more suffering for themselves and others due to the illusion of mind.

This compassion comes with no feelings of superiority but from the sincere wish for all to be free from their mind-created-self so that they can live happier lives. The only thing that makes me feel better or superior would be my mind-created-self and that isn't real remember? I am the same as all other people in the sense that I have been tricked by my mind and I am also the very same conscious energy underneath. We are all the same emotional beings, no better; no worse, just perfect conscious energy that has limitless potential. If only everyone could see this then there would be happiness for all.

This is the beginning of true compassion.

Compassion

When one whom I have benefited with great hope
Unreasonably hurts me very badly,
I will learn to view that person
As an excellent spiritual guide.

Verse six

In short, I will learn to offer to everyone without exception
All help and happiness directly and indirectly,
And secretly take upon myself
All the harms and suffering of my mothers

Verse seven

People are controlled by their mind-created-self so it's no wonder that we will experience people who abuse a helpful hand. We should not view them in anger or disappointment because they are only acting in a way that they believe will make them happier. The cause of their suffering is the same that creates the negative feelings we may have towards them.

If we view them with hate or anger then they should be equally entitled to hate us. We cannot blame them unless we also blame ourselves for our negative thoughts, feelings and actions because they are born from the same illusion of mind.

Instead we should feel compassion for anyone who *'trespasses against us'* (The Lords Prayer) because they search for happiness in all the wrong places. We should be thankful to them for reminding us of the sufferings caused by the mind and use their negative actions as a kindly test to strengthen the control over our own mind.

In this way, we can say that the person who; *"**Unreasonably hurts me very badly**"* should be seen *"**As an excellent spiritual guide**"*.

This reminds me of Jesus, who after being betrayed by one of his closest companions and horrifically abused by deluded people, he still showed great compassion by saying:

*"**Forgive them father, for they know not what they do**"*.

Like a mother whose love does not waver when her child is having a tantrum. The mother does not see her child as bad or evil when they behave badly because she recognises that the child is merely acting irrationally due to their deluded mind. What the child is upset about is made highly important to them because of their self-grasping mind. Like the eyes of a mother on her child, Jesus knew that his persecutors were not to blame for the actions of their mind-created-self.

It is said that Jesus was once hit in the face by a deluded man, and instead of retaliating, Jesus felt total compassion and offered him his other cheek.

If a person hits us with a stick, we would not blame the stick but the person wielding it. Likewise, when a person behaves badly towards us, do not blame them but their deluded mind that wields their words and actions.

This doesn't mean that we should never stick up for ourselves of course and certainly does not mean that we should let people take advantage of our compassionate nature. It means that we act in ways in which does not cause further harm or unhappiness to others. Be constantly mindful of how inappropriate actions are based on a false concept of self and feel compassion for that person in the knowledge that they are suffering needlessly. If their actions do not harm anyone's spiritual growth then consider offering:

... to everyone without exception
All help and happiness directly and indirectly,
And secretly take upon myself
All the harms and suffering of my mothers.

We should feel compassion for all others because they are slaves to the delusions of mind and do not see the precious jewel underneath the dirt they are desperately protecting. Their minds create a worldview that sees themselves as separate, a world that has them in the centre and they grasp and attach themselves to material things. We now know that none of these things will create happiness for them.

Recognising the synonymous nature of ourselves and all beings with love and compassion we can create a sincere wish for all life to be free from suffering and wish for them to see the true nature of all things.

Our mind has been created and nurtured in a materialistic and disconnected world, it can therefore be hard to view the human race as being inherently compassionate. So, to help us see the world with compassionate eyes we should realise that without others we would have nothing at all.

It is due to the intentional and unintentional kindness of others that we were born, born safely, fed, clothed, nurtured, sheltered, got jobs, got paid, had holidays and felt the love of friends and family. Without the help from other people in a giving and receiving relationship, we would not be here. Without giving and receiving with compassionate minds the ripple of happiness will not spread.

Why are we here?

That's the big question, why *are* we here?

What if I said that our goal and purpose in life is to become immortal? Yep, "immortal", why not?!

If we completely get rid of our mind-created-self and free ourselves from all material attachments, including our own physical body, our conscious energy is free to exist wherever it pleases. If our consciousness is not attached to our body, then when our physical being comes to pass, our consciousness is not held by the mind and thus, we do not die per se.

If we have truly become enlightened and are unimpeded by attachments of the physical, then we can be free to manifest our consciousness as anything we choose. We may choose to put our energy into another human life to be born again. This incidentally, is why there have been fourteen Dalai Lamas. It's the same conscious being, choosing to reincarnate as a human for the good of all living beings.

Once you return to the universal energy source free from worldly attachments you can choose to help enlighten other beings as you see fit. It may be that you decide to remain as the universal energy and help influence the energy produced by those people in prayer, or those who need guidance in life.

Indeed, most of what you wish for comes true, so could it be that past enlightened beings are helping you, helping to bring you things to aid your spiritual growth and happiness?

What's the point in life? To become free from the restrictions and sufferings caused by mind-created-self and thus, become free to return to the universal energy source so that you can be eternally happy and free to help others achieve the same.

In this sense therefore, we are God. We are all God in the sense that we are all the same energy source and have the power to influence and help all beings. Perhaps this is what Jesus meant when he said: *"God is within you"*.

You may not be in the right place or time to believe in this, and that's ok. Just to have a general awareness or basic appreciation of this concept is a step towards your own enlightenment.

Lets try and back this up with a bit more science. Scientists weighed terminally ill patients at their moment of death to find that at the very moment the patient stopped living and all consciousness and worldly attachment had left them, their weight dropped by twenty-one grams. Taking all things into account, the scientists have no idea where this weight loss comes from or goes to, but I have an idea. Baring in mind that physics tells us that energy cannot be created or destroyed but can only move from one form to another; could our true consciousness, the wave energy that is our true self weighs twenty-one grams?

At point of death, the life force or energy is no longer needed and therefore, moves from one form, out of our physical body, back into the universe until it is caught up into another cycle. If the conscious energy has made the most of their life and has freed their energy from the material world then they have no more connection to the physical world and are free to choose how best to reincarnate their energy for the good of all living beings.

Science shows that we are made up of nothing but energy and therefore, we cannot 'die' as such but we will move into a different form. This is the concept of reincarnation. All you have to do is dump your mind-created-self (it serves you no helpful purpose anyway) and set free the conscious energy and rejoin yourself with the universal consciousness of all things. This is why some Buddhists leave all belongings behind them in the pursuit of enlightenment because they know that they have no need for any of it. They leave their family and all their possessions to dedicate their lives to become enlightened, to rid themselves of all attachments created by their mind and to directly see their true self as synonymous with the universal energy of all things. They sacrifice all they have because they realise that they have an amazing opportunity as a conscious, thinking human being to become enlightened and rid him or herself of the constant suffering of reincarnation. Those choosing this path are know as Bodhisattvas and they decide to sacrifice all physical attachments because they are able to truly appreciate the enormity of their opportunity as a human. They understand that a small degree of suffering and hardship in this life will be minuscule in comparison to the life times of sufferings, stuck in the cycle of reincarnation. If they don't make the most of their life as a human and become enlightened, then they wont have the control over the direction their conscious energy takes when they die. Bodhisattvas understand that if they don't make the most of their human life and become enlightened, then their energy will remain attached to the physical world and they may spend many lifetimes suffering horrifically, perhaps as a fly, a beetle, flee, dog or cat. Such creatures and animals have unimaginable sufferings and do not possess the opportunity to learn and become enlightened like a human being. It may take many thousands of lifetimes to be reincarnated as a human again so Buddhists who decide to become an active Bodhisattva decide to take full advantage of their opportunities whilst they have it.

If you're still not convinced yet because this thought is a little bit too *"far out man"*, it's not surprising because, lets face it, it's completely the opposite to what we have been brought up to believe. We have been brought up to believe that we are separate from all things and that we are living beings that perish and die. Some believe that in the end there is a heaven and a hell. What could be more hellish then spending eons being reincarnated as a fly, a beetle or a bird that live off foulness and have none of the comforts of human beings? Heaven on the other hand would be being free from this endless suffering, free from mind, free to exist as part of the universe and able to help all other beings.

Is it so hard to believe? After all, it wasn't so long ago that we believed the earth was the centre of the universe. It wasn't so long ago that we believed the earth to be flat either. Science proved us wrong in both cases and now we can accept that the world is round and our planet is one in a galaxy of thousands.

Let me ask you this question then: Where does the universe end? There's our galaxy and the thousands upon thousands beyond that, but where does it end? And if it ends, what's outside that? These are questions that our mind knows must have an answer but cannot comprehend the enormity of it because it has experienced nothing like it. We know that life ends. The road ends. The day ends. A hole we dig in the garden ends. All things we have experienced haven't equipped us with the tools to understand the concept of an eternal universe. Similarly, even though science is showing us that we are not solid and that there is an alternative reality to the one our minds have us see, we find it very hard to understand and formulate. This does not mean that it is not true however. I have an open mind. Open yourself up to the possibility that what is written here is true and if it is, then life has a point to it and there is no limit to what we can achieve for ourselves and ultimately for every single being.

So, to get back to the question: why are we here? Who knows why or where the universal energy came from originally and perhaps that fits in with some of your own religious beliefs, but what I do know is that if you want it, you can live in the knowledge that you cannot truly die. Whilst you are waiting around to change from one form of energy to another, you can manifest everything you want for yourself by tapping into the universal energy source and moreover, if you choose a Bodhisattvas path, you can create endless opportunities for everyone else too.

You are everything, and everything is you so live, love and laugh to the fullest and thoroughly enjoy the gift of life.

Some things have no purpose so, what's the point?

We act compassionately towards others because we are mindful that everyone is suffering due to their tricks of mind. By remembering that the mind is nothing more than an amalgamation of experiences and doesn't truly exist, we should also act with patience and compassion because we cannot know the motives behind peoples' actions.

Left unchecked, our mind-created-self is free to grow strong and manifest unhappy emotions such as anger even at the most insignificant problems in life. Not only does anger hold no purpose but also its existence is usually based on conjecture, pure guesswork and assumption of the mind.

For example; a man drives into a busy supermarket car park. The only space he finds is impossible to get into due to the angle and position of the car parked in the adjacent space. The man gets very angry at the inconsiderate parking. At this moment the owner of the poorly positioned car returns and with rage the angry man aggressively confronts him about his thoughtless parking.

However, as it turns out, the reason why the gentleman had parked at such an angle was due to the car that was parked in the now unoccupied space. It was not his parking skills that caused upset but someone elses. Now that the original car had moved on, it looked as though he parked badly.

This is a good example of how we make leaping judgements and assumptions on people, their actions, words and behaviour. The only thing we can be a hundred percent sure about is that our own mind-created-self will cause us to be upset with others.

No one of their right mind enjoys being upset. There is no pleasure in having negative emotions such as anger within us and yet we often hold onto it, as if to savour the upset. Some times we even feed it with further angry thoughts to keep it alive, to fuel it into rage or hate. We even fuel our anger for many hours or even years after the cause has long passed. Eventually however, we let the anger fade and we naturally forget about it.

What's the point in holding onto something that causes nothing but nasty feelings and negativity in our lives, when it will eventually disappear anyway?

We get angry at something and then the anger eventually disappears. If such unhappy emotions serve only to cause us and other people more sorrow, and if the state will disappear away in the end anyway, why not just let go as soon as it arises within us? We have total control over such horrible emotions and its only our mind-created-self that keeps it alive by going over the situation. So, get rid of anger because there really is no point to it.

Being angry is not pleasant for others or ourselves, and it's certainly not healthy for our mental and physical state, so why bother nurturing it? Instead why not let it go immediately.

Anger is a common emotion and one that holds absolutely no positive benefits to anyone.

Even in competitive martial arts such as boxing, as soon as one contender becomes angry, all technique disappears and they will soon lose the competition. Interestingly, the concept of having *"no mind"* is the underlying principle of all martial arts. Having a state of 'no mind' means being completely present in the moment and thus, having no mind-created-self to disrupt focus and clarity with thoughts and emotions. This is why martial arts is often associated with spirituality, balance of body and mind and peace-of-mind.

The reason why we get angry with others is usually unfounded because we can never be sure of the motives behind their actions. Moreover, if a person is being harmful towards us, we know that they would not act in such a way if it were not for their deluded mind and we should remember that they are expressing their own suffering.

Patience is the enemy of anger and impatience its ally

Invest in the physical and mental health for yourself and those around you by destroying all anger through the practice of patience.

"Practicing the principle of an eye for an eye, leaves everybody blind"

Mahatma Gandhi

Practice patience whenever confronted with situations that previously created anger within you. Always be mindful whenever anger begins to show its ugly head and be patient in the knowledge that it will go eventually so why not get rid of it immediately.

Anger holds absolutely no purpose on the road to happiness so let go of that baggage today.

What goes around comes around.

Buddhists believe that the actions you do in this life affect what happens to you in the next life. Jesus also said: *"Do unto others as you would have done unto yourself"*. I'm sure so many other religious and spiritual texts state similar karmic laws.

Knowing that we are all connected and that we are all part of the same soup of energy, it makes sense that if we take what is not ours, then we are effectively taking from ourselves. Energy cannot be created or destroyed remember. All things want to balance and return to a state of equilibrium. Send out negative energy through your actions and the balance will be restored when the negative energy finds its way back to you.

As we are energy, we can see how the principle of Karma fits with Sir Isaac Newton's law, which states:

For every action, there is an equal and opposite reaction

To be honest, it doesn't matter whether you believe in reincarnation, past lives, religion or any of that stuff to believe in the laws of Karma because we have all experienced Karma directly or indirectly.

Karma works like an unwritten universal law and tends to 'pay back' our intentional negative actions by taking away the very things that we have tried to gain for ourselves.

Far from being some sort of cosmic mumbo-jumbo, in its simplest form, Karma is something that we can all understand clearly and perhaps have seen in our own lives.

For example: it makes perfect sense that if we act in deceitful or spiteful ways in an attempt to increase our own social status or popularity, we can expect to end up receiving the exact opposite. Attempting to gain popularity at the expense of other people will drive people away from us and we receive loneliness and unpopularity in return. This is Karma.

If you continually steal from others to gain material things for yourself, you can eventually expect to find yourself in jail with very little, and all your goods taken from you. Again, you will end up with the exact opposite to what you attempted to gain. This is Karma.

If you continually cheat on the ones that love you, or use other peoples affections with flippant disregard to gain physical pleasures for yourself, then eventually you will end up unloved and most likely find it very difficult to keep any meaningful relationship. This is karma.

If you continually take from other peoples kindness with a greedy mind for your own selfish gains, then you cannot expect to continue to receive such kindness and you will once again, receive the opposite from what you believed you were cunningly getting. For every action there is an equal and opposite reaction and therefore you will have to give back kindness unselfishly in order to regain peoples trust. This is Karma.

In its simplest form, this type of action and opposite reaction is Karma. Karma therefore also works on the positive too. If you are kind, caring and give to others with a compassionate mind, you will receive an abundance of comforts in return.

Knowing about Karma, but choosing to continue to act selfishly, is like a man with 20:20 vision walking straight off the edge of a cliff. It is crazy behaviour.

In the bible it says: *"do unto others as you would do unto yourself"*. This is Karma.

Some people are kind people and yet seemingly negative things happen to them. Firstly, you can never know what a persons intensions are. Kind acts may have selfish or unkind intensions. Secondly, remember that negative things are happening due to the karma created from your own actions. Negative things will happen in your life and you can choose to frame it by viewing yourself on the effect side of life and that life is being cruel to you, or you can see the hurdle as a challenge, an opportunity to learn and grow. But most of all, see your challenges in life as an opportunity to pay back your negative Karma and thus, recognise that you are moving one step closer to having no negative Karma at all.

Look back over your life and think about your behaviour. See if you can identify occasions that might be the cause of your current Karmic situation. Relax though; be mindful of your actions and the words written in this book. Start to pay back your negative Karma today by showing compassion and giving happiness to others. When rubbish things occur in your life, reframe the situation and know that it will pass. It may be a very tall order at the time but try and refocus on the grand scheme of life and know that you are paying back karma and therefore, you are taking a step closer to lasting happiness.

Be wise

We're nearing the end of this book and we've talked about all sorts of things from the delusions and illusions of mind-created-self, the importance of meditation, entanglement, the power of the HERE and NOW and all manner of wonderful things. But all of these concepts would mean very little without a little pinch of wisdom.

An enlightened or 'awakened' mind cherishes others above itself and holds a sincere wish for all others to be happy. But an enlightened mind is also a wise one. The practice of giving and receiving MUST be accompanied with wisdom.

It would be utterly foolish to lay down our lives just because someone asked us to but it may be wise to do so if our sacrifice helps spread the ripple of happiness to many others.

Isn't this the concept of Jesus dying on the cross? Jesus laid down his own life and forgave all those that trespassed against him because he knew that his death will improve the happiness and install compassion into millions of people for many years to follow. This is ultimate compassion with wisdom.

All Buddha's and Bodhisattvas sacrifice their own comforts so that they can be free to help spread compassion and help save all beings from harm and suffering.

A compassionate man once found a fish on the side of the road, which had fallen from a cart. Through compassion for the fish, he picked it up and released it into a near by pond. A few weeks later the villagers realised that all but one large fish were dead. The villagers realised that the mans seemingly compassionate actions of saving the fish from the roadside had resulted in the suffering of many other fish when it ate them all!

Although the man had saved the fish out of compassion, compassion alone was not enough and without wisdom, acts of kindness can backfire.

The basic rule is that we should not give or take anything from someone if it does not aid his or her happiness or your own spiritual growth. For example, if someone asks for a book, give it to them gladly and without attachment to it. However, if someone asks for your religious text which you rely on for your own spiritual growth you should decline.

The good intensions of giving a homeless person some money may enable them to by drugs or alcohol. This is not wisdom because it will not help them to be happy. However, give them the coat on your back and you provide them with warmth and a small degree of happiness.

Similarly, if someone continually hurts or upsets you to the point where your own spiritual growth and ability to spread happiness is being effected, then it is wise for the good of all parties to leave this person and never return.

Be wise in your actions and think about the results and consequences of your behaviour. Be mindful of how your compassionate actions can be of help to your own and other peoples spiritual growth.

Summary:

Who or what created the universal consciousness in the first place is for you to decide but what this book shows is that there is no God who has control over your destiny but 'God', in this sense, is a universal energy that you and all things are undeniably linked to and connected with. This makes you a little piece of 'God'.

Through prayers, meditation and even simple wishes, you are focusing your drop of energy onto the universal ocean of energy and thus, you create a ripple which has the potential to bring you what you want in life. Like sending an order by post and then sitting back and waiting for your goods to arrive, you can manifest things for yourself.

There is nothing wrong with wanting things for yourself, after all, if you aren't happy then how can you expect to make others happy. However, use this power wisely and be mindful of Karma. If you wish to create something for yourself, ask double for other people. If you want something for yourself, see if you can combine your wish to give something to other people too.

The ultimate gift for yourself and all beings is to become fully enlightened. Destroying your worldly attachments by slaying your mind-created-self will bring you everlasting happiness and the ability to provide the same for all beings too.

It is only your mind-created-self that prevents you from seeing the real world around you. Through meditation, compassion, selflessness and mindfulness within your day-to-day actions, you will diminish its strength and set free the real you. The real, perfect and jewel-like you which you were born into this world as, is not obsessed with living in the future or the past but recognises them as illusions of the mind. The true life we are living is happening in the present moment, the constant of HERE and NOW. This recognition creates a worry free existence and one that lives life to the fullest. You will not be around forever in the physical sense and who knows if you will get this chance as a conscious human being again, so do not cherish materials and possessions because they will all turn to dust along with your own body. Make the most of what is real in life such as the present moment; spend your days focusing on what is important like your connection with all things and the power of positive energy such as compassion and love.

Once we diminish or even destroy the mind-created-self and all its subsequent illusions, you will recognise the pointlessness of the negative emotions we harbour and therefore, identify them as having absolutely no purpose but to cause harm.

Anger, jealousy, greed, lust, spitefulness and hate are emotions based on a self-cherishing mind that actually does not even exist.

With the knowledge gained from these realisations you should also understand why others act negatively and feel compassion for them, as you would wish them to feel for you. See yourself in others and develop a strong desire to help them be happy as if you were wishing it for yourself because we are all the same in many ways.

We are all connected and we are all part of the same universal soup of energy. There is nothing that separates you from any living thing.

Therefore, if, through greed, jealousy or hate, you take from other people, you are in effect, taking from yourself and the negative energy you have put out will have consequences in your own life. This is Karma and you should always be mindful of it. It is not God punishing you or some judgmental "All Mighty" but simply the laws of physics. We are energy and for every energetic action there is an equal and opposite reaction.

Basic rules:

1. Do not be fooled or ruled by the illusions and delusions of mind. Be mindful of all your thoughts and actions so that you can destroy all negative ones before they have a chance to destroy happiness.

2. Meditate to free the real you and create some headspace.

3. Whatever you put in your mind will grow, so reframe negative thoughts and become addicted to positives ones.

4. Always remember that you are not separate from any living thing. Through wisdom, treat all beings with the utmost respect and compassion.

5. You create your own reality. You are connected to all things so sit back. Be thankful for what you have today and enjoy receiving the things that you will receive tomorrow but do not become attached to them.

6. The present moment is the true life so live in the HERE and NOW often. The future and past do not exist. Be aware of the horizon but know that you will never reach its end so enjoy the grass beneath your feet as you walk towards it, otherwise your journey will be wasted.

7. Challenging things occur in life, so accept it as Karma and as an opportunity to repay the dept. Ironic though it is, by being mindful of repaying Karmic dept when naff things happen, you should be aware that you are taking a step towards lasting happiness. Do not dwell on the challenges that life may throw your way. Don't be a victim but reframe the situation into a positive or simply relax in the knowledge that it will pass. Chances are it will turn out to be a necessary hurdle to get you or someone else onto greener pastures anyway. This is Karma.

So, What's the point?

You are potential energy and hopefully you now recognise that your potential is far greater then you could have previously imagined. Believe in the truth that energy cannot be created or destroyed but only moves from one form onto another. Who knows if, or when your energy will come in the form of a conscious being again, so make sure you live with love and compassion in your heart, learn to grow and remember that words are the signposts, so now it's time to start walking the path. Every journey begins with a single step so even small steps are moving you forwards. Be mindful of the journey, because that's where life takes place.

Put down all your negative baggage so you can travel light.

Enjoy the movie of your life because it is the most amazing story ever to be told.

Nameste

Anthony Peters

Eight Verses on Thought Transformation

(i)

With a determination to accomplish
the highest welfare for all sentient beings,
Who surpass even a wish-granting jewel,
I will learn to hold them supremely dear

(ii)

Whenever I associate with others, I will learn
to think of myself as the lowest among all,
And respectfully hold others as being supreme,
From the depth of my heart.

(iii)

In all actions, I will learn to search into my own mind,
And as soon as an afflictive emotion arises,
Endangering myself and others,
I will firmly face and avert it.

(iv)

I will cherish beings of bad nature,

And those oppressed by strong negativities and sufferings,

As if I had found a precious treasure

Very difficult to find.

(v)

When others, out of jealousy, treat me badly

With abuse, slander and so on,

I will learn to take all loss

And offer the victory to them.

(vi)

When one whom I have benefited with great hope

Unreasonably hurts me very badly,

I will learn to view that person

As an excellent spiritual guide.

(vii)

In short, I will learn to offer to everyone without exception

All help and happiness directly and indirectly,

And secretly take upon myself

All the harms and suffering of my mothers.

(viii)

I will learn to keep all these practices

Undefiled by the stains of the eight worldly conceptions,

And, by understanding all phenomena to be like illusions,

I will be released from the bondage of attachment.

Lightning Source UK Ltd.
Milton Keynes UK
UKOW050146180113

205047UK00001B/50/P